'Pick any letter at random – you'll laugh every time' – Tom Bowler

'Cookin' – Sue Chef

'Side–splitting' – Ben Dover

'You'll wet yourself laughing' – I. P. Freely

'Each letter is more outrageous than the last' – Shirley Knot

'The perfect stocking filler' – Mary Krismass

'Kept hiccupping in hysterics!' – Pat McBak

'Henby really wrapped the wool over their eyes!' – Ivanna Nitt

'This guy could get away with anything!' – Laura Norder

'A hoot' – Gray Owl

'A winning book' – Jack Pott

'Hilarious – I couldn't stop crying!' – Anita Tissue

'Couldn't put it down' – Paige Turner

'I applaud the stars for surviving Henby's wit' – Holly Wood

# DEAR CELEBRITY

## Absurd Letters to the Stars

Written and illustrated by

Julian Henby

First published in 2008 by Capstone Publishing Ltd. (a Wiley Company) The Atrium, Southern Gate, Chichester, PO19 8SQ, UK. www.wileyeurope.com

Email (for orders and customer service enquires): cs-books@wiley.co.uk



*Other Wiley Editorial Offices*
John Wiley & Sons Inc., 111 River Street, Hoboken, NJ 07030, USA
Jossey-Bass, 989 Market Street, San Francisco, CA 94103-1741, USA
Wiley-VCH Verlag GmbH, Boschstr. 12, D-69469 Weinheim, Germany
John Wiley & Sons Australia Ltd, 42 McDougall Street, Milton, Queensland 4064, Australia
John Wiley & Sons (Asia) Pte Ltd, 2 Clementi Loop #02-01, Jin Xing Distripark, Singapore 129809
John Wiley & Sons Canada Ltd, 22 Worcester Road, Etobicoke, Ontario, Canada M9W 1L1

Wiley also publishes its books in a variety of electronic formats. Some content that appears in print may not be available in electronic books.

A catalogue record for this book is available from the British Library.

Library of Congress Cataloging-in-Publication Data
Henby, Julian.
Dear celebrity : absurd letters to the stars / written and illustrated by Julian Henby.
p. cm.
ISBN 978-1-906465-23-0 (pbk.)
1. Letters--Humor. 2. Celebrities--Correspondence--Humor. I. Title.
PN6231.L44H46 2008
808.81--dc22

2008031723

ISBN: 978-1-90646-523-0

Typeset by Sparks, Oxford – www.sparkspublishing.com
Printed and bound in Great Britain by TJ International, Padstow, Cornwall

Substantial discounts on bulk quantities of Capstone Books are available to corporations, professional associations and other organizations. For details telephone John Wiley & Sons on (+44) 1243-770441, fax (+44) 1243 770571 or email corporatedevelopment@wiley.co.uk

# DEDICATION

To Mum
(who supported me in this project
even though she didn't always approve)

To Dad
(who would have enjoyed my book
and who I wish was still around to do so)

# CONTENTS

# Henby Family Tree

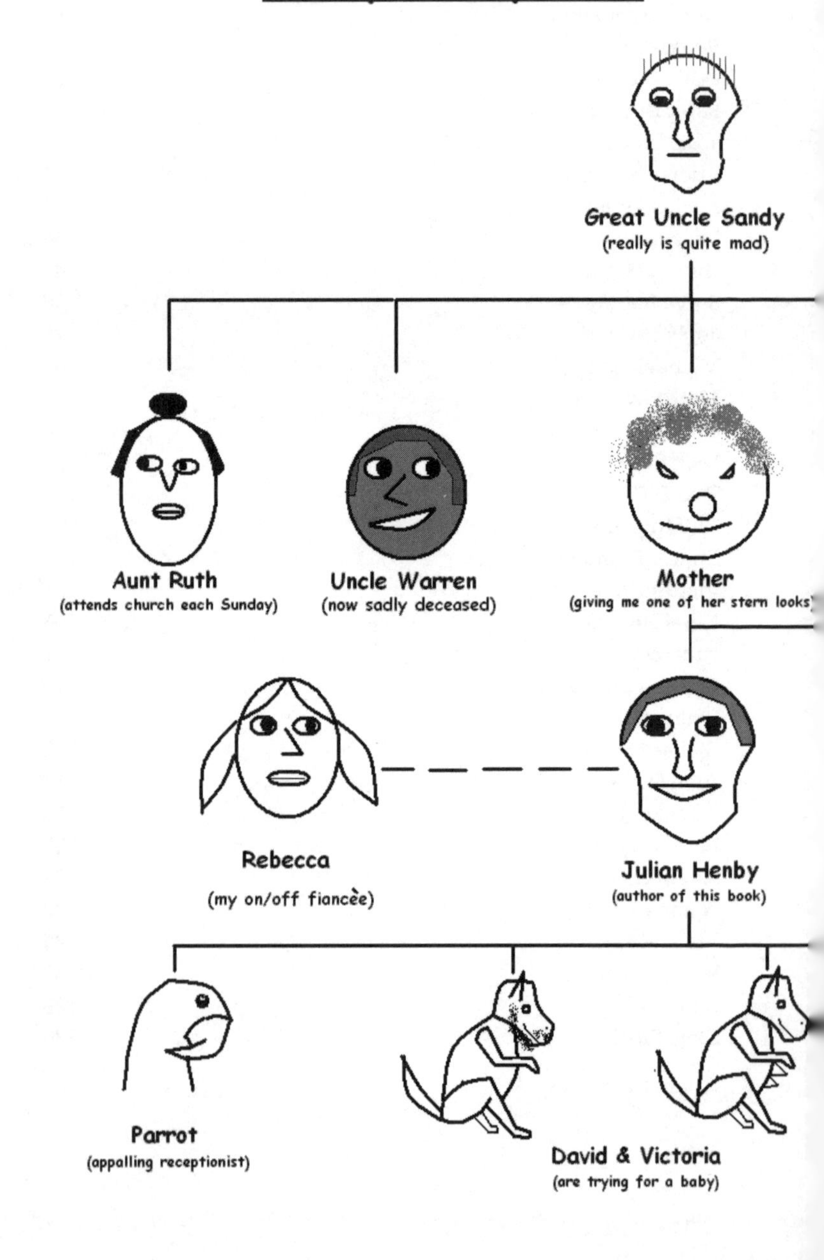

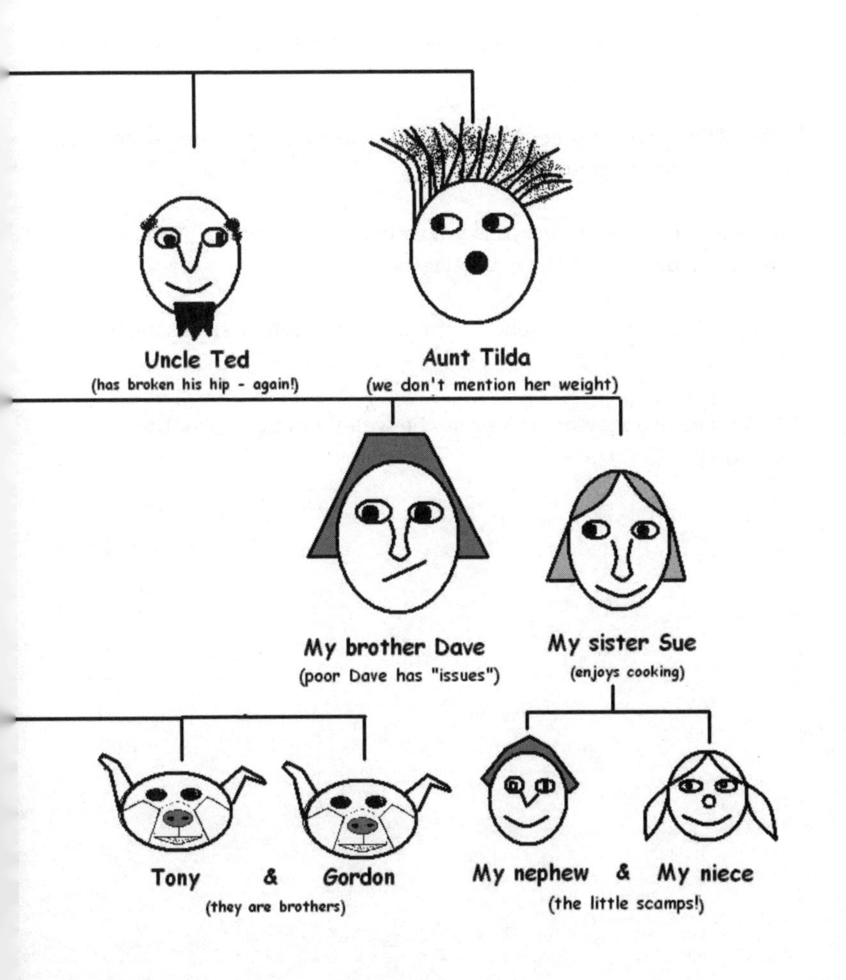
Uncle Ted
(has broken his hip - again!)
Aunt Tilda
(we don't mention her weight)
My brother Dave
(poor Dave has "issues")
My sister Sue
(enjoys cooking)
Tony
&
Gordon
(they are brothers)
My nephew
&
My niece
(the little scamps!)

# ACKNOWLEDGEMENTS

Many thanks to my friends the I.L. staff at Ernest Kleinwort Court who spent hours stuffing letters into envelopes. Apologies for the paper cuts but at least I supplied the sweat and tears.

Special thanks to my friend Lee Saunders for his contribution.

Thanks to my friends who read my early letters and encouraged me to continue.

Thank you to my brother Nicholas for the feedback that influenced the book to a great extent.

Sincere thanks go to everyone who replied to my letters. Without them this book would have been rather sad.

Finally, I wish to thank Robert Popper whose brilliant books inspired this one.

All proceeds go toward replacing the wall-padding in poor Dave's bedroom.

Flat 12
Burgess Hill
West Sussex

29 November 2006

Sir Jimmy Savile OBE
Aylesbury

Dear Sir Jimmy

My brother (Dave) is convinced that he is you! The trigger for this delusion seems to have been his messy divorce last year. Ever since then Dave has been wearing lots of heavy, gold jewellery and a track suit. He never smoked before but he now gets through several luxury cigars each day. He has also taken to an intense regime of jogging each morning which the doctor says is not good for his heart, and the jewellery weighs him down too, straining his joints. He insists that he's training for a marathon.

Dave has also started talking in a strange voice and makes a silly noise at the beginning of each sentence (which can be infuriating). He also keeps saying, 'now then, now then, now then, jingle-jangle, jingle-jangle' which irritates me immensely. Perhaps more worryingly, he has been threatened with the sack from the telephone call centre where he works if he doesn't 'snap out of it'.

The psychiatrist can't seem to help much.

Do you know of anyone else suffering from this affliction (apart from yourself)? If so, what sort of treatment do they require?

Yours truly

Julian Henby

Julian Henby

SIR Jim IS THE Loch Ness Monster. So there !!

ONLY 700 MILES FROM DAVE !!!

Flat 12
Burgess Hill
West Sussex

16 January 2007

Sir Jimmy Savile OBE
Aylesbury

Dear Sir Jimmy

Many thanks for kindly sending me a signed photo bearing the note that makes reference to my brother Dave. I am sorry to say that Dave's condition has deteriorated in recent days and I blame myself.

My grave error was to give him the photo you sent me. My hope was that the picture would force him to face the truth: that he is *not* Sir Jimmy Savile. Instead, Dave now believes himself to be the mythical 'Loch Ness Monster'. Over the past few days, Dave has been spending most of his time at the *Sussex Yacht Club*, snorkelling in the lake and scaring the sailors. Yesterday, he was nearly hit by a motorboat that had to swerve to avoid him, crashing instead into a yacht. Dave was arrested by the police and has now been banned from the *Yacht Club* premises.

Dave also insists that he is visible only when partially submerged in water. He is seeing the psychiatrist next week and we expect him to be admitted to hospital.

Many thanks for trying to help. It is now clear that Dave requires the full support of a psychiatric team.

Yours truly

JH

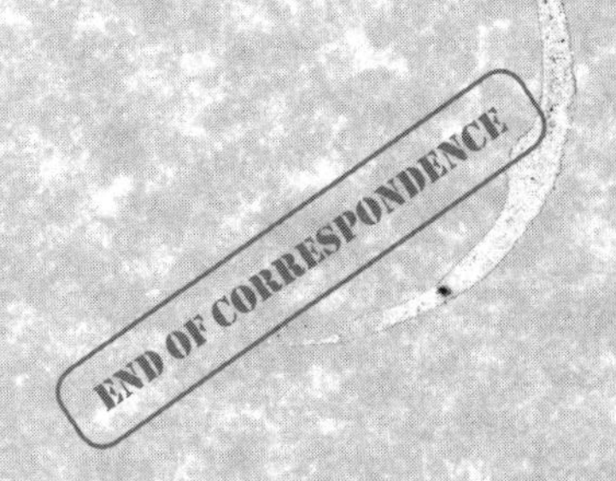


Julian Henby

Flat 12
Burgess Hill
West Sussex

25 October 2006

Mr Damien Hirst
London

Dear Damien

Firstly, let me say that I am a huge fan of your artwork. I particularly enjoyed the piece for which you took three politicians, skinned them alive and placed them in a life-sized replica of the House of Commons. I am sure we would all like to strip away the façade of lies and half-truths behind which these people so often hide.

But, I must get to my point. For many years I have harboured a deep desire to be an artist and express myself through abstract representation. However, my school art teacher once forced me to eat a clay-sculpture I had made, accusing me of banality. The sculpture was of Barry White and it made rather a big meal. Since then I no longer have the stomach to produce anything artistic.

So, last week I made a momentous decision: If I can't be an artist I will *become the art itself!* I admire your use of organic materials and I would like to offer you my own bodily organs for use in one of your pieces. I rarely seem to make much use of my toes (especially the smaller ones) so I would be willing to donate two from each foot. Similarly, I could do without two fingers from each hand. In addition, I have calculated that I could lose eight teeth without ruining my smile. One ear could be replaced by a prosthetic (although I require the other one for listening to my *Meat Loaf* CDs). I would like to preserve my sense of smell, but I could sacrifice one nostril for the sake of art. I agonised over whether to donate an eye, but eventually I decided not to – sorry Damien (you see, I am trying to persuade my fiancée Rebecca to live with me again, and she has always liked my eyes). That's about all I can afford to donate apart from hair, one kidney, bodily fluids and, of course, my appendix.

I imagine you employ your own surgical team. However, I am able to save you this cost because my uncle used to be an orthopaedic surgeon before his license was revoked a few years ago; he has agreed to remove all parts to be donated (but I must send Mother on holiday first so we can use the bathroom).

Please let me know how you wish to obtain the materials – I can either drop them off or post them to you if you prefer. Also, are there any parts you do *not* want?

I look forward to being included in your exhibition. Please let me know the name of the piece comprising my body parts so I can come and see it.

Yours truly

J. Henby

Julian Henby

Flat 12
Burgess Hill
West Sussex

13 October 2006

Mr Huw Edwards
c/o BBC News
London W1A 1AA

Dear Mr Edwards

I write to you for help with a very delicate matter.

My fiancée (Rebecca) and I experienced some difficulties with our relationship in the spring of last year. Things seemed to come to a head when I deliberately started to eat bananas again after many years of abstinence, despite knowing this particular fruit provokes in me a very unpleasant allergic reaction. This was the final straw for Rebecca and she moved out of my flat.

Unable to cope on my own, I tracked Rebecca down to beg her to come home. I dragged a bag of my laundry to where she was living. All my clothes had changed colour in the wash and were ruined. I posted each garment through Rebecca's letterbox and implored her to come back before my entire wardrobe was devastated!

Unfortunately, the police were summoned and I was arrested. And, to make matters worse, there was a court hearing that resulted in the worst possible ruling: *I am not allowed contact of any kind with Rebecca*.

I cannot risk further brushes with the law, but I must contact Rebecca before insanity takes hold. I therefore ask for your help.

At the end of a forthcoming edition of the 10 O'Clock (evening) News, please make the following announcement:

'This is a message for Snugglebunny from Bananabum. I'm sorry and I need you back. I love you. Please phone my mobile.'

Rebecca never misses the 10 O'Clock News and I am confident she will understand the message. Hopefully, the average viewer will not even notice the announcement. Please let me know when the message will be broadcast.

Yours truly

J. Henby

NO RESPONSE

Julian Henby

Flat 12
Burgess Hill
West Sussex

3 October 2006

Michael Jackson
London
EC1M

Dear Michael

I paid an agency quite a lot of money to find your address – I hope you don't mind. I was surprised when it turned out to be a UK address instead of American, but I suppose a superstar like you probably has houses all over the world.

I am so excited to be in contact with you. I have been following you for the past nine years and I'm a huge fan of your work. I think you're so talented.

Please could you send me a signed photo of yourself. I'll be moonwalking all around town when I receive it.

Keep on thrilling us, Michael. You're the greatest!

Yours truly

Julian Henby

Julian Henby

MICHAEL D JACKSON
MARKETING MANAGER

London
United Kingdom

Flat 12

Burgess Hill
West Sussex

6 October 2006

Dear Julian,

Thank you for your letter of 3 October. I'm afraid that the agency you paid has come up with the wrong Michael Jackson!

I am a 33 year old marketing manager in an independent arts and heritage publishing company with the same name (although he's Michael Joseph Jackson and I'm Michael David Jackson, so I'm not a perfect match), but alas none of the musical talent! I've attached my business card in case you want to contact the agency that tracked down my contact details and get your money back – perhaps they were confused by the central London address into thinking he'd bought a property here.

Anyway, I wish you luck in your search for Michael Jackson superstar. Perhaps you could reach him via his official website which should list his UK fan club address?

Best regards,

Michael

Michael D Jackson
Marketing Manager

Flat 12
Burgess Hill
West Sussex

Mr Michael D Jackson
Marketing Manager (not singer)
London

Dear Michael

Many thanks for your letter of 6 October explaining that you are in fact Michael David Jackson (marketing manager) and not Michael Joseph Jackson (the king of pop).

You said in your letter that you have none of the musical talent of the other Michael Jackson. But, come now Mr Jackson – I'm sure you can bang out a good tune when you think no one is listening. I bet you can even do a Moonwalk (be careful if you try this in the shower because I know from bitter experience that you can slip over and crack your coccyx).

I doubt the agency will refund my money. However, you are quite a close match to Michael J Jackson. Would you consider sending me a signed photo of yourself dressed as the other Michael Jackson and singing along to 'Billy Jean'? At least then I can honestly say I have a signed photo of Michael Jackson.

Good luck with the marketing management.

I look forward to hearing from you.

Yours truly

Julian Henby

END OF CORRESPONDENCE

Julian Henby

Flat 12
Burgess Hill
West Sussex

15 January 2007

Mr Des O'Connor
London

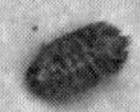

Dear Des O'Connor

I am an enormous fan of yours, especially your music. Indeed, my great admiration for your work has prompted me to set up a new Des O'Connor Appreciation Society, now boasting ten recruits!

This Appreciation Society differs from most others because we intend to take a distinctly direct approach. My belief is that it is imperative to express one's appreciation directly to the subject, making good use of pomp and showmanship. We have therefore designed a regime of celebrations that we intend to perform on a daily basis (every day except Christmas Days). The regime is as follows:

At 7.00am, members of the Des O'Connor Appreciation Society will begin to march toward your road, accompanied by a brass band. As they march, the band will play the tune to 'Des Is Great, Des Is Good' (a song that has been written especially for the Society). The brass band will be led by a group of six cheerleaders carrying a banner bearing the Society's name. The musical procession will take approximately two hours to make its way through the streets that lead to your road.

At 9.00am, the procession will enter your road. Having reached its destination the band will continue to play, marching on the spot for a further hour. You are encouraged to come to your upstairs window to acknowledge and watch the procession.

At 10.00am, you will be collected at your door by a young female model. You will receive a golden crown before being seated on an ornate wooden throne that will then be lifted aloft by four of our members. The band will resume playing your special song and marching on down the road with you held high – the king of light entertainment. The procession will take the pre-determined route through the town, attracting members of the public to its number all the while.

At 2.00pm, the procession will be approaching your road once again. Your throne will be lowered and your crown removed. A dapper man wearing a bowler hat, bow-tie and white gloves will show you to your door. At this point we bid you farewell until the next morning! The brass band etc. will then continue marching and playing until it reaches the agreed debriefing point some five miles away.

Before starting our services to you we require some vital information. Please let me know your address and when you would like us to start.

Yours truly

J. Henby

Julian Henby

NO RESPONSE

Flat 12
Burgess Hill
West Sussex

15 January 2007

Mr Rod Stewart
London

Dear Mr Rod Stewart

I am developing a new cologne for older men – a process that is now entering its eighth year. The bulk of my work has revolved around researching the role of the human pheromones that have a major role in an individual's ability to attract sexual partners.

My research suggests that a small percentage of older men produce a unique pheromone that is highly effective at attracting the younger woman. We have found that this chemical is emitted only by this group of men (all over sixty) and is only effective on younger women (aged 18-25).

However, to be conclusive our research requires a much larger sample of volunteers. We are therefore in search of older men who are known to attract only women in the 18-25 age bracket. The aim is to carry out tests to determine whether these men produce the unique pheromone.

We feel that you are an ideal candidate for this study and we therefore invite you to take part. The process will involve a simple questionnaire and a sample of perspiration. It will take only a few hours and we will pay you for your time.

Please let me know whether you are able to participate and when you would be free.

Yours truly

NO RESPONSE

Julian Henby

Julian Henby

Flat 12
Burgess Hill
West Sussex

9 October 2006

Mr Brian Blessed
London

Dear Brian

You will recall that last Christmas you made an appearance in Brighton's main shopping mall. I cannot remember whether you were there to recite poetry or something else, I suppose it was something like that. What I do remember quite vividly is that you wore a sheep-skin lined red robe (or dressing gown) with a matching hat, and your many fans were lining up to see you.

I was with my nephew when we saw you (my nephew is six). He was very keen to meet you so I took him to the little tent you had erected in the mall. Later, he emerged beaming and holding a small gift you had given him for Christmas. You are a very generous man, Brian, and I thank you for making my nephew's day.

Do you have any plans to appear at Brighton again? Is it something you do every Christmas? Please let me know – I would love to take my nephew to see you again (I will caution him not to expect another present).

I look forward to hearing from you.

Yours truly

JH

Julian Henby

Julian a lovely Letter. deeply appreciated! Unfortunately I won't be in Brighton this year.

Flat 12

Burgess Hill
West Sussex

9 October 2006

**Private and Confidential**
Mr Brian Blessed, Honorary President

Dear Brian

You will recall that last Christmas you made an appearance in Brighton's main shopping mall. I cannot remember whether you were there to recite poetry or something else, I suppose it was something like that. What I do remember quite vividly is that you wore a red robe (or dressing gown) with sheep-skin lining, and your many fans were lining up to see you.

I was with my nephew when we saw you (my nephew is six). He was very keen to meet you so I took him to the little tent you had erected in the mall. Later, he emerged beaming and holding a small gift you had given him for Christmas. You are a very generous man, Brian, and I thank you for making my nephew's day.

Do you have any plans to appear at Brighton again? Is it something you do every Christmas? Please let me know - I would love to take my nephew to see you again (I will caution him not to expect another present).

I look forward to hearing from you.

Yours truly

JH
Julian Henby

Please give my Love & Best Wishes to Your Nephew! Merry Xmas! Brian Blessed o! Ho! Ho!

Flat 12
Burgess Hill
West Sussex

24 November 2006

To: Professor Lord Robert M Winston

Dear Professor Winston

I am writing to you because you are a world authority on fertility and highly respected in your field. I have seen many of your television programmes and enjoyed them very much.

My two gerbils (David and Victoria) have been trying for a baby for some time now without success. Of course, they have not told me that they are having problems (they can't talk), but their behaviour makes this crystal clear. They seem to have some sense of romance because they usually make love when the sun is setting. I also often hear them at it during the night when I am in bed: their running-wheel rattles and their cage knocks against the wall, then I hear David let out a little groan. It is terribly sad for me to hear them trying so hard night after night without success and this is really getting me down.

Recently, I felt so desperate that I decided to try artificial insemination. After a long search on the internet I found some raunchy photos of rodents making love in a variety of settings and outfits. I showed these pictures to David in an attempt to excite him and tried to collect any proceeds in an egg-cup. My plan was to extract the stuff from the cup using a syringe which I would then use to transfer it to Victoria. However, the photos did little for David and there was nothing to collect. Of course, there was no guarantee of success even if the procedure had been completed: I am concerned that David might be firing blanks. A few months ago I was attempting to put him in the cage when he slipped from my hand and caught his nether-regions on a sharp part of the cage. Perhaps this accident has ruined his prospects.

I would very much appreciate your help, Robert. May I bring the gerbils to your clinic for treatment? How much will it cost?

Your truly

Julian Henby

Julian Henby

|  |  |
|---|---|
| **From :** | Robert Winston |
| **Sent :** | 15 February 2007 16:25:27 |
| **To :** | "Julian Henby" |
| **Subject :** | Re: Please Help IN STRICT CONFIDENCE |

Dear Mr Henby,

I was extremely sorry to hear about David and Victoria's difficult problems and the obvious distress which their attempts at conception are causing.
I do think though you are going about this in totally the wrong way. There are several issues which come to mind.

1. Forgive me for being completely blunt, but has it not occurred to you that gerbils greatly value their privacy. You surely have observed the method by which they dive into warm dark places when nesting. They may not be able to talk, but the fact that they know you are listening to them in their most intimate moments in that prurient way is really rather shocking. It is not all surprising that David lets out a little groan occasionally; I am surprised at your lack of sensitivity. I would strongly recommend that you immediately rehouse them in a remote, soundproof area well away from where you sleep. And I would recommend that you keep the G pornography for your own purposes rather than challenge what is clearly a very close relationship.

2. If David really cannot achieve an erection – erectile insufficiency is virtually unknown in Gerbillinae (I assume David is from Africa rather than from the more delicate Asian species. I presume he is not of Russian origin Rhombomys opimus – the great gerbil not called 'opimus' without reason?), then why not try a small amount of Sidenafil in his water supply. If you give me the body weight of David, I could calculate the most appropriate dose – but possibly a few scrapings from a single 50mg tablet of sildenafil (Viagra) would be more than enough. You certainly do not want priapism which is very inconvenient (and potentially extremely painful) in a gerbil trying to exercise on the bars of a treadmill

3. Have you considered Victoria more carefully? Once, I had two rabbits from Harrods sold to me as females – this deceit was only uncovered when they 'tried to get pregnant' but both were male but it was a shock when I realised; it could just be that D & V are enjoying a slightly unusual sex life. but now, I guess, with the government's latest plans, they could always adopt, I suppose.

Best wishes
Robert Winston

Flat 1
Burgess Hi
West Susse

16 February 2007

To: Professor Lord Robert M Winston

Many thanks for your expert advice regarding David and Victoria. It is quite obvious that you really know your stuff.

Your point about the poor gerbils needing their privacy seems very valid and something I hadn't considered before. But it makes perfect sense.

I have taken your point very seriously. David and Victoria now occupy the spare bedroom where there is no risk of being observed by voyeurs like me.

I am not sure whether David comes from Russia or Asia (I have been listening for an accent in his squeaks but to no avail). However, I 'borrowed' a Viagra tablet from my grandfather (who is 104) and fed David a few scrapings as you suggested. David promptly became erect and tried to chase Victoria around the cage. The trouble is, David's locomotion was severely impaired by his erection which dragged along the floor like a fifth leg (I think he's suffered s friction burn). Further, poor Victoria seems terrified by David's sudden virility and I think she may be severely traumatised. David now seems permanently aroused while Victoria cowers in the corner of the cage.

It seems their sex life is more problematic than ever! What am I to do now, Professor Winston?

Yours truly

JH

Julian Henby

END OF CORRESPONDENCE

Flat 12
Burgess Hill
West Sussex

15 January 2007

Mr Nick Baker (wildlife expert)
London

Dear Nick

Due to some rather detrimental genetically acquired traits (such as clumsiness and stupidity), I have found myself unable to hold down gainful employment of any kind. As a last resort, I have decided to throw caution to the wind and start my own business!

There is a long tradition of chimney sweeping in my family and I have decided to carry on the trend. Of course, there has not been much call for this service in recent years, but I am confident that there are sufficient active chimneys in the country to make a viable business.

According to the RSPCC, the practice of sending one's children up the chimneys to clear out the soot is now considered bad form. This revelation has scuppered my plans for a truly family run business and my nephew (who is six) is terribly disappointed about the cancellation of his job offer. However, I am not prepared to allow bureaucracy to defeat me – where there's a will there's a way!

And I have now discovered that *way*. Following an extensive search on the internet, I eventually found a parrot for sale in Cornwall. This would be the perfect solution to my problem: although small, bipedal and very vocal the parrot surely could not be considered a child by the RSPCC.

I have now obtained the bird which is safely installed in my spare room, awaiting enrolment on my staff training programme. The trouble is, I suspect I shall be forced to rewrite the manual for the parrot and I must confess that this task has me rather flummoxed.

Knowing that you are a renowned expert on birds, I am writing to you in the hope of procuring some advice. When training such an unusual worker, where does one start?

I would be most grateful for any guidance, and I look forward to hearing from you.

Yours truly

NO RESPONSE

Julian Henby

Flat 12
Burgess Hill
West Sussex

20 October 2006

Sir Patrick Moore
Gloucestershire

Dear Sir Patrick

I have been an amateur astronomer for some fourteen years. I try to look at the sky with my *Celestron 8 Inch CPC Schmidt-Cassegrain* telescope every night (unless Mother gets it into her head that I am practicing some kind of devil worship, then I have to stop).

Anyway, I was star gazing last Tuesday night at about 2.00am when I saw something unusual. In fact, I am convinced it is a brand new planet. It was brown and blue with (I think) at least one moon in orbit.

May I send you a picture of my discovery?

Yours truly

Julian Henby

Julian Henby

**Sir PATRICK MOORE** ***CBE. FRS.***

Oct 27

Dear Mr. Nenby,

I am sure that this wasn't astronomical.But I wi'l certainly look aftt it if you like.

Sincerelt

Flat 12
Burgess Hill
West Sussex

3 November 2006

Sir Patrick Moore CBE, FRS
West Sussex

Dear Sir Patrick

Many thanks for your letter of 27 October regarding my discovery of a brand new planet. Thank you for offering to look at the planet – I would be honoured if you would.

I am so excited about my discovery. All those years peering into the telescope were not in vain after all! I will be submitting my notes and sketch to *New Scientist* as well as the astronomy magazines for publication. This is certain to be big news all over the world.

Would it be OK with you if I say that I was working in association with you to uncover the planet's secrets?

I look forward to hearing from you soon.

Yours truly

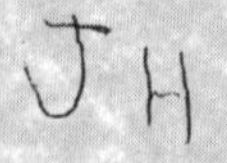

Julian Henby

enc

# brand new planet

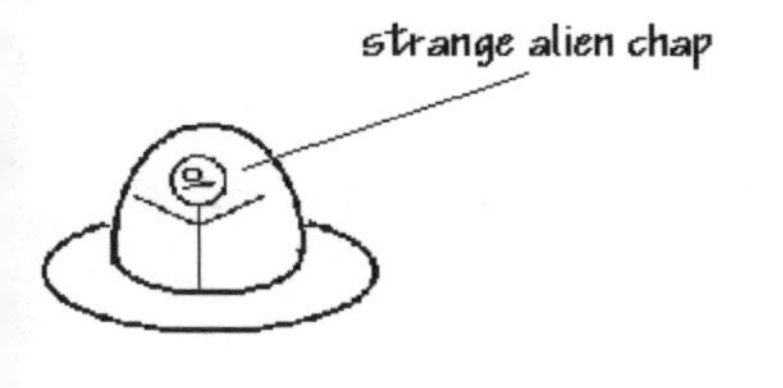


(I may have imagined the aliens or they may have had different space craft)

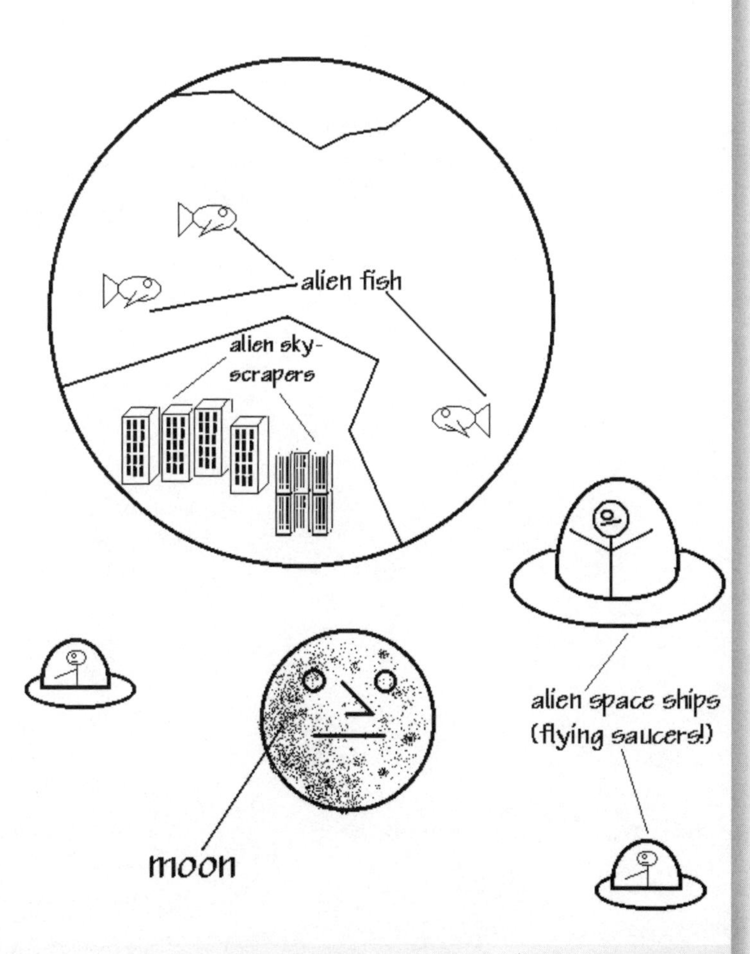

**Sir PATRICK MOORE *CBE. FRS.***

I hate to be a wet blanket - but I must be honest. I don't know what you are seeing, byt I am 100% certain that it is not astronomucal .... Flying saucers and aliens are great fun, but, I fear, fictional.

Please do NOT associate me with this!

Believe me, with best wishes

Sincerely

Patrick Moore

Flat 12
Burgess Hill
West Sussex

18 November 2006

Sir Patrick Moore CBE, FRS
West Sussex

Dear Sir Patrick

Many thanks for your recent letter regarding the planet that I thought I had discovered.

This is terribly embarrassing to have to admit, but I am afraid I have made a very silly error. You see, it turns out that my brother (Dave) had been messing around with my telescope a few weeks ago and managed to smear his mascara onto the lens. Stupidly, I neglected to clean the lens before using it, so what I took to be a planet was in reality a combination of *Max Factor* makeup and an over-active imagination. I discovered the mascara mark only yesterday and I managed to extract a confession from Dave by threatening to tie-dye his favourite wig.

I feel absolutely wretched for wasting your time over this; I do hope you have not endeavoured too much to find the phantom planet. You must think me an awful amateur.

To make this whole mess even worse, I have appointments with the editors of several international science/astronomy magazines to sell the story of my 'momentous discovery'. I have arranged to meet each editor at a different time but all on the same day – next Wednesday! What should I do, Sir Patrick? I feel such a fraud!

I can see only one way out. I think I shall have to go and stay with my uncle in Canada, at least until this all blows over. Also, I think I will have to leave my parrot behind so it will need a good home (in case you're interested).

I am a cursed blemish on the face of astronomical research!

Yours truly

JH

Julian Henby

**Sir PATRICK MOORE *CBE. FRS.***

November 22.

Dear Mr. Henby,

Well done - I fell for it!

Of course I knew that it wasn't a planet, or anything astronomical, but I thought I was dealing with a genuine crank . I can usually spot this sort of thing, but this time I didn't, and I admit defeat.

Give my love to the Niagara Falls!

All good wishes

Sincerely

Patrick Moore

Flat 12
Burgess Hill
West Sussex

29 November 2006

Sir Patrick Moore CBE, FRS
West Sussex

Dear Sir Patrick

I regret to inform you that Mr Henby has embarked on a tour of Canada and is not expected to return to the UK for several months
*Aaaaark!!*

Kind regards

Pretty Polly *aaaaaark-aaaaaark!!!*
PA to Julian Henby

END OF CORRESPONDENCE

Flat 12
Burgess Hill
West Sussex

16 February 2007

Mr Noel Edmonds
London

Dear Noel

I have been a big fan of yours since the days of *Swap Shop* when you adorned my television screen with your gaudy pullovers. I write to you for expert advice.

I am aware that you are a helicopter enthusiast and even hold a pilot's licence. I too am very interested in aviation, particularly helicopters. I hope to obtain a pilot's licence like you one day, but for now I must settle for radio controlled models. I recently purchased a *Predator Gasser SE* radio controlled helicopter which I enjoy flying in my local park. Despite a few minor accidents, there have been no fatalities and I feel I am developing into a very skilled pilot.

Anyway, I must get to the point. My two gerbils (David and Victoria) recently had a litter of babies after several months of trying. We are all thrilled, of course, and I feel they deserve a special treat. So, I am in the process of organising a helicopter ride for David, Victoria and the babies across the Sussex Downs. I estimate the flight will last about one hour and involve a number of daring stunts including looping the loop, stalling and weaving between power cables. The *Predator Gasser SE*'s cockpit is full of mechanical hardware, allowing no room for passengers, so I have built an extension on the top to accommodate the gerbils (it looks odd but should be functional – see enclosed diagram).

This is something of a first, both for me and the gerbils, so there are a few unknowns. One of my concerns is the effect of G-force. Please could you advice me on ways of minimising the effects of this on the gerbils? I will also take the precaution of administering motion-sickness tablets. Is there anything else I should take into consideration?

I would be grateful for any advice you can offer.

Yours truly

Julian Henby

Julian Henby

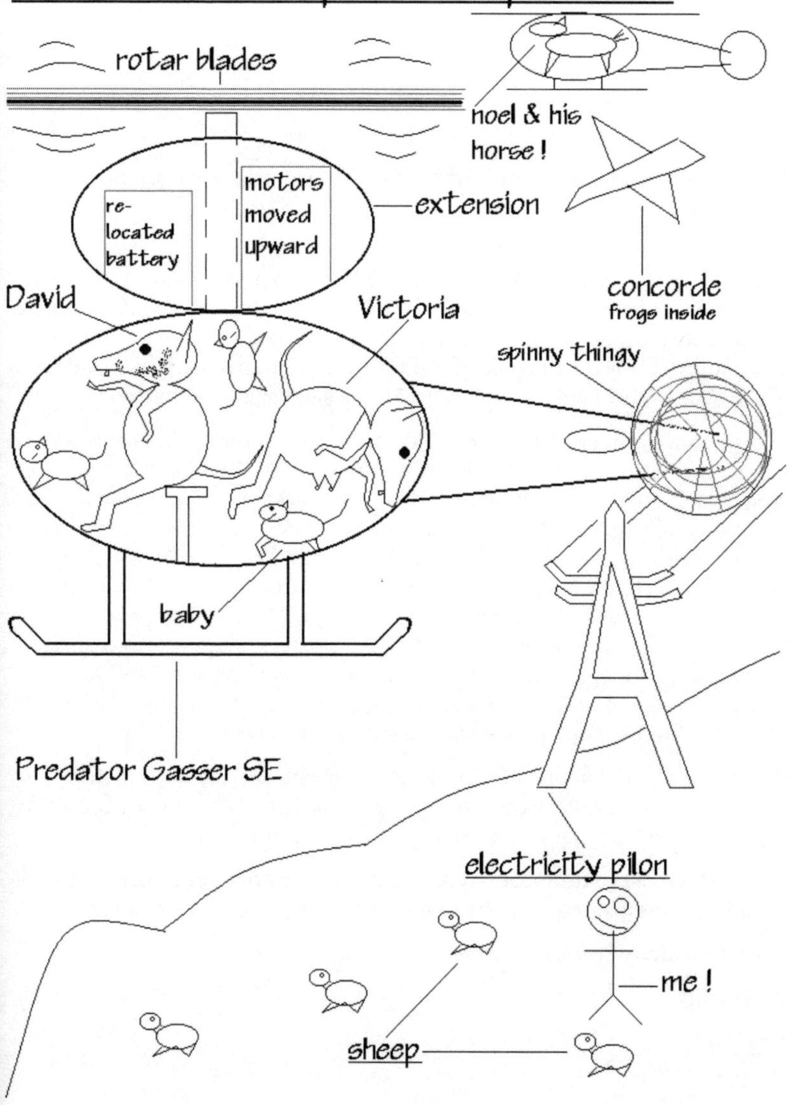
David & Victoria's Special Helicopter Ride !
rotar blades
noel & his horse !
re-located battery
motors moved upward
extension
concorde
frogs inside
David
Victoria
spinny thingy
baby
Predator Gasser SE
electricity pilon
me !
sheep

Flat 12
Burgess Hill
West Sussex

8 July 2007

Mr Michael Flatley
London

Dear Mr Flatley

A few years ago I saw your show *Lord of the Dance* and was totally entranced by it.

My uncle Ted is currently recovering from a stay in hospital and surgery after falling over and breaking his hip. The doctors have advised him to do some gentle exercise every day but old Ted is rather a lazy chap and refuses to get active. Unfortunately, his recovery has been slower than expected and I suspect this could be attributed to his rather torpid lifestyle. But who could blame him? I mean, exercising for the sake of it is boring!

This insight has inspired a new project that I am working on. I have been conducting a tour of the orthopaedic wards of all the hospitals in my area, speaking to elderly patients who are being treated for broken bones sustained during a fall. These people are all invited to join my 'music and dance' group upon their discharge from hospital. The group has just one ultimate goal: to perform *River Dance* before a large audience. Such an exciting goal is just what is needed to motivate these elderly people to exercise their bodies as prescribed by their doctors. Since starting my tour of hospitals I have recruited 27 members who practice your *River Dance* for six hours per day. Seven members have temporarily dropped out due to fresh falls but we hope to welcome them back after their surgery.

What we need is a venue for our big performance and my hope is that you may be able to advise us on how to secure such a theatre slot. Perhaps you would even be in a position to offer us some contacts.

I would be most grateful for any assistance. Let us not forget that this is all designed to help our elderly people swiftly to recover from serious injury.

I look forward to hearing from you.

Yours truly

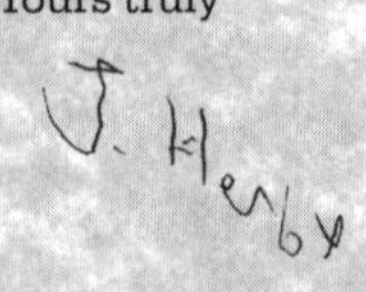

NO RESPONSE

Julian Henby

The Stardust Club
Flat 12
Burgess Hill
West Sussex

8 July 2007

Ms Sophie Ellis-Bextor
London

Dear Sophie

I own a night club here in Sussex. I am such a big fan of yours that I have devoted a whole room of the club to you and your music. The room is called *The Sophie Ellis-Bextor Room* and designed around your song *Murder On The Dance Floor*. Our dance floor is decorated with red spatters depicting puddles of blood and the bloody footprints of a murderer. In one corner of the dance floor the victim is slumped with a knife protruding from her chest – a faithful representation of Miss Ellis-Bextor herself rendered in wax. Lurking in every dark corner of the room is a suspect, skulking in a suspicious manner. These mechanical dummies can move and speak in a spooky way while your song echoes around the walls like a ghost.

We hope to open the *Sophie Ellis-Bextor Room* in the Autumn and I would be most honoured if you would kindly come along and cut the ribbon. It looks like being a very well attended event and we are laying on a buffet for our loyal guests.

Please let me know when you would be free.

Yours truly

**NO RESPONSE**

JH

Julian Henby

Flat 12
Burgess Hill
West Sussex

30 October 2006

The Private Bill Office
House of Commons, London

Dear Sirs

I recognise the need for politicians of different parties to conduct a robust debate when wrestling with a controversial issue such as what colour to paint the parliamentary ladies toilet. However, my feeling is that your colleagues often flout the rules of common courtesy when referring to one another's policies and feelings often get trampled under the boot of arrogance. This makes for distasteful television viewing and leaves a bitter taste in one's mouth.

To rectify this problem whilst preserving the means for healthy debating, I have devised a set of protocols for your inter-party dealings, especially those that occur in the glare of the media. To be effective, my protocols must become legally required standards, maintained by all party politicians. I will now outline just a few of my proposals.

Whenever two rivalling politicians meet (whether in public or not) they must take turns to give each other a 'piggy-back' over a distance of no less than 500 yards. If infirmity or physical feebleness prevents them form doing this, they must feed peeled grapes to each other instead.

For every negative remark that a politician makes about another politician, that politician must follow this with three sincere compliments about his/her colleague.
Example: *'His foreign policy is incompetent, but he makes heavenly fairy-cakes, he has a beautiful singing voice and he keeps his skin soft and supple.'*

Before concluding any encounter between one and other, politicians must each kiss the other on the cheek and whisper something loving in his/her ear.

When communicating via telephone, it would be an offence for any politician to be the first to hang up at the conversation's conclusion.

The full list of protocols is described in a document I am calling 'The Courtesy Bill'. This document is 309 pages long and would legislate for all aspects of communications between politicians to ensure these are conducted in a respectful, loving manner.

Please inform me of the correct procedure for submitting a new bill to parliament or the House of Lords.

(I am willing to become your new Minister of Courtesy.)

Yours truly

Julian Henby

Julian Henby

THE PUBLIC BILL OFFICE
HOUSE OF COMMONS
LONDON SW1A 0AA

Mr Julian Henby
Flat 12

Burgess Hill
West Sussex

3 November 2006

Dear Mr Henby.

Thank you for your letter of 30 October regarding a bill on the subject of protocols governing the way in which politicians conduct themselves.

I can advise that the matters you wish to see regulated by legislation are more suited to the internal rules of the House and Codes of Conduct for Members than to primary legislation. A private bill - and I note that you rightly addressed your letter to the Private Bill Office – would need to be brought forward by promoters, who engage Parliamentary Agents in order to draft the legislation and advise on its passage through Parliament. This is not a straightforward (or cheap!) business but I am afraid that there is no other way for a private individual or organisation to bring forward legislation.

A more general Bill governing standards of behaviour might be brought forward by a willing Member as a Private Member's Bill but I can envisage a number of practical difficulties in framing the type of legislation you seem to have in mind in a viable way.

Nonetheless, your thoughts are of interest and relevance.

Thank you for taking the trouble to write.

yours sincerely

**Chris Shaw**
**Public Bill Office**

Flat 12
Burgess Hill
West Sussex

15 January 2007

Mr Hugh Grant
London

Dear Mr Grant

I am a great admirer of your films and I consider you to be one of my favourite British actors. What is particularly admirable, I feel, is that you have achieved enormous success as a film actor despite suffering from a severe stammer. In fact, this is what has inspired me to follow my dream of pursuing a career in film!

You see, from a very young age I have longed to work as an actor, but I have been hampered by a condition the symptoms of which are similar to *Tourette's Syndrome*.

Over the past decade, I have had many disastrous auditions. My first audition was for a part as a vicar in a television drama. Unfortunately, the director felt that my character was unlikely to shake his fist at God and hurl a barrage of abuse at Jesus in the middle of a wedding, so I did not get the part. Years later I finally managed to land a job in a stage production of a Shakespeare play. My performance inspired the newspaper headline: 'Bard Turns In Grave As Foul Mouthed Hamlet Turns The Air Blue'.

If only I could find a role that would be enhanced by my condition! Last month I thought I had found the perfect part when I auditioned as a drunken vagrant. On this occasion my tendency towards profanity and gibberish was positively beneficial. However, I found myself involuntarily speaking dialogue meant for my fellow actors so even this audition ultimately failed.

As an actor, you succeeded against all the odds and are therefore in an excellent position to offer me some guidance. How am I to make it in this ruthless business? I would be most grateful for your help.

I look forward to hearing from you.

Yours truly

JH

Julian Henby

**NO RESPONSE**

Flat 12
Burgess Hill
West Sussex

15 January 2007

Mr George W Bush
The White House
Washington, DC

Dear Mr President

I am British and very patriotic. However, I have been a big fan of you and your politics for some time. I congratulate you on all the good work you have been doing.

Here in the UK we have a very popular children's television presenter called Basil Bush. He is always very dapper and has the air of rusticity about him. I am most curious to know whether Basil is related to you in any way as there does seem to be some resemblance.

I would be most grateful if you would kindly take a moment to answer my question. It is one of those things that has been bugging me.

I look forward to hearing from you.

Yours truly

Julian Henby

Julian Henby

NO RESPONSE

Flat 12
Burgess Hill
West Sussex

17 November 2006

Mr Bill Oddie
Hampshire

Dear Mr Oddie

I am aware that you are an expert on birds and write to you for advice on a very difficult matter.

I am in the process of going into business, designing and marketing a range of costumes for sale via fancy-dress and other types of store. Launching the business with a very limited capital, I have been forced to cut some corners. Indeed, it has become apparent that we cannot afford to employ a full-time receptionist to take customer enquiries and orders via telephone. This is potentially a disastrous problem and the business will collapse if a solution cannot be found.

By some stroke of luck I happened to view a television programme about parrots recently. As most people know these birds are capable of human-like speech, and this gave me an idea. After a long search I found a suitable parrot for sale and purchased the bird with the intention of training it as my receptionist.

The trouble is, the bird is not as keen to learn as I had been led to believe. My first task was to familiarise the parrot with the basic functions of our telephone. It's a speaker-phone so it is just a question of pressing the correct buttons. However, after several days of intensive training the parrot was managing to accept incoming calls only about 25% of the time. However, worse was to come: On one occasion, I discovered the incompetent bird had used speed-dial to telephone my aunt who mistook the bird's squawks for the screams of a crazed intruder. Fearing I was about to be massacred by the lunatic, she called the police and I ended up having to explain the whole business to bewildered officers at the local police station.

Having put that embarrassing incident behind us, I turned my attention to training the parrot to speak so that it could answer telephone enquiries and take orders. Together, we listened to interminable broadcasts by BBC Radio 4 and audio books. I read Charles Dickens and Shakespeare to the dumb bird but even such literary masters could not inspire it to find the power of speech. Eventually, the parrot learned a few short phrases such as 'Speak, damn you!'; 'Press receive! Receive!'; 'Thick creature!'; and several crude expletives. These are hardly the phrases becoming of a professional receptionist.

Why does the parrot mock me so? Mr Oddie, I turn to you in desperation. Please offer me some advice.

Yours truly

JH

Julian Henby

Mr Julian Henby
Ernest Kleinwort Court
Oakenfield

12TH July 2007

Dear Julian,

Thank you for your letter to Bill Oddie which he has asked me to reply to on his behalf.

I think all of us have at one time or another had to deal with a receptionist whose sole aim in life is to turn away all calls. It seems you have found and trained one that instead of requiring a salary will cheerfully accept being paid in peanuts!.

I can't see how your particular parrot will enhance the reputation of your business but you never know. Perhaps if you posted a video of it on the internet you could generate a John Cleese hotel owner like following for your business – it would certainly be a different approach.

Best wishes

**Douglas Batchelor**
Chief Executive

Printed on re-cycled paper

Flat 12
Burgess Hill
West Sussex

15 January 2007

Mr Richard Briers
London, W1W

Dear Mr Richard Briers

Three years ago, I watched a few episodes of your television sitcom *The Good Life*. It was the first time I had ever seen the programme and I must say I found it inspirational.

In fact, the show had such an effect on me that I decided to get out of the rat race and move to the countryside where I would be self-sufficient. Marching uninvited into my boss's office, I dumped a bag of manure onto his desk. 'No more sales reports. This is my bread and butter now', I told him. He could stick his fat pay cheque – I didn't need it anymore!

Six months later I had bought a small cottage in Cornwall and was attempting to grow a range of vegetables in the spacious garden. My plan was to grow enough produce not only to sustain myself but also to make a good living at the local market. I also purchased some hens for laying and hoped to make a profit selling the eggs to my neighbours. To say that things failed to go to plan would be an understatement!

Most of my crops failed to grow, apparently due to 'the wrong sort of soil'. I did, however, succeed in growing some marrows which were desecrated by a neighbour's satanic dog that went on the rampage and broke through my fence one night. Attempting to sell the damaged vegetables at the market, I referred to the teeth-marks as 'a decorative feature' and was promptly reported to the Trading Standards Agency. My reputation as an honest farmer was then mud, of course. Reasoning that a bit of male company would encourage my lacklustre hens to lay, I introduced them to a rooster. The upshot of this was that an embryo was found in a customer's breakfast.

Days later, I was run out of the village by a mob of angry country folk brandishing a range of farming implements. This all seems a far cry from *The Good Life*.

I feel your television programme misled me badly. If I had refrained from watching it I would now have a job, I wouldn't be broke and I wouldn't be in this stinking hole of a flat.

How can you defend this sort of irresponsible programme making? I look forward to hearing from you.

Yours truly

Julian Henby

Julian Henby

Dear Julian
What an awful time you had all because of our little show.
About 30/40 people did try "THE GOOD LIFE" but I did say on various media that life would in fact be dreadful, working from dawn to dusk for very little profit.
Most of the couples dropt out – a few stayed and survived.... just.
I was very glad I was just an actor!
I only hope you are NOT too old to make a fresh start in something that gives you pleasure and a decent living.
I offer humble apologies and all possible luck for the future

Sincerely

Richard (BRIERS)

Flat 12
Burgess Hill
West Sussex

15 February 2007

Mr Richard Briers
London

Dear Richard

I received a letter from you yesterday. I can tell you that it came as an unexpected but very pleasant surprise! When I read your letter I could hardly believe that it had come from the one and only Richard Briers! I have been a big fan of yours for many years and particularly enjoyed *The Good Life*.

Now I have a confession to make, Richard: I do not know what your letter is referring to. Presumably, you wrote in response to a letter from me to you, but I am afraid I don't recall writing to you!

Do not be alarmed by this, Richard – the problem is entirely at my end. You see, a little while ago I moved to Cornwall in the hope of starting a new life. The idea was to become self-sufficient by growing my own vegetables. Unfortunately, there was a disagreement with a local farmer which resulted in my head getting beaten with a spade! After a stay in hospital, I decided to move back here to Sussex, and once I had settled it became apparent that the assault on my head had destroyed my short-term memory! The wretched thing causes so much confusion and so many misunderstandings!

Well, your letter certainly is very kind and I thank you very much for it.

I wonder whether you would be kind enough to explain to me what our correspondence was all about.

Yours truly

Julian Henby

Julian Henby

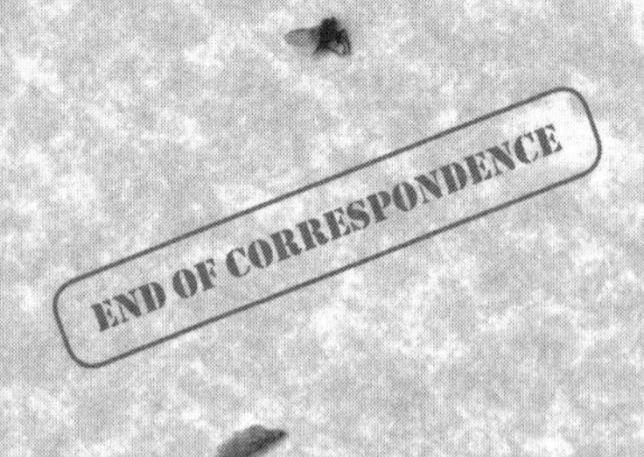

Flat 12
Burgess Hill
West Sussex

22 January 2007

Professor David Bellamy O.B.E.
London

Dear David

I have fond memories of watching the natural history television programmes in which you are apparently shrunk to the size of an ant to observe tiny creatures and plants. Of course, this was just a camera trick.

I write to you because I have discovered a way of being shrunk to the size of an ant – for real! I know you must think me mad, but I swear this is true. The discovery was made when I visited a nightclub in Basingstoke recently. There, I met a young man who sold me a small tablet that he said would open my mind. I could not have imagined the awesome power of this tablet!

Ten minutes after ingesting the tablet I felt myself shrinking. Several seconds later I was the size of an ant, peering up at the towering people around me. Initially, this was terrifying but I gradually started to enjoy it. I decided to explore the great outdoors where I met a family of friendly caterpillars, got chased by a spider and flew on the back of a moth. It was amazing.

Sadly, within four hours I had returned to my normal size and was floating in a pond.

I feel this tablet could be the key to a revolution in scientific research! Doctors could become miniaturised so that they could enter a patient's body and carry out surgery. And professionals within your field of work could explore the lives of tiny creatures – for real!

This is indeed an exciting discovery. I have written to several scientific magazines and expect the story to break worldwide soon. You heard it here first!

Would you have any objection if I report that I am working together with you to identify the best applications of this new drug?

Yours truly

JH

NO RESPONSE

Julian Henby

Maximum Security Prison
Burgess Hill
West Sussex

21 November 2006

To: Mr Uri Geller

Dear Uri

I have a contact on the outside who claims it is possible to bend metal using only your mind, and he says that you (Uri Geller) know how to do it. My contact has seen your television shows and is confident that you will be able to help me.

Apparently, you use psychic powers to bend spoons. If this is true, you should be able to bend metal bars in the same way. Since being in prison I have become an artist; I produce sculptures. For my next work of art I would like to fashion a set of solid metal bars into a sculpture. However, I do not have access to the equipment needed to bend the bars.

Would it be possible for you to impart the secrets of using psychic powers to bend metal (specifically bars)? I would appreciate it if you could visit me during visiting hours and tutor me on the 'black arts'.

Please let me know when you are free.

This is top secret, Uri. Please tell nobody. When you visit me, please say you are my uncle and say nothing about the tutoring.

Yours truly

JH

Julian Henby

Printed: 02 February

**From :** Uri Geller from my BlackBerry
**Reply-To :**
**Sent :** 02 February 2007 18:21:39
**To :** "Julian Henby"
**Subject :** Re: Attention Mr Uri Gellar

Hi julian thanks for your offer but I moved on and not interested but art always was my passion good luck with your work. Much energy uri

Flat 12
Burgess Hill
West Sussex

29 January 2007

Rt. Hon. Mr John Major (former PM)
London

Dear Mr Major

Firstly, let me say that you are one of my favourite living Tory former Prime Ministers: you truly are.

I will now turn to the subject of my letter. It is well known that you love peas and simply cannot get enough of them. In fact, I read in a reputable tabloid newspaper that you compulsively consume garden peas at regular intervals throughout the day and have even had your garden converted into one big field for growing peas! I must say, I admire your dedication.

For some time now I have been producing a very successful range of home-made pickles which are selling like hot cakes at my local market. Last year, I decided to expand my stall by adding a brand new product and your love of the humble pea has inspired me to make this my new item. Following your example, I created a field and harvested a bountiful crop of peas.

The peas are sealed inside air-tight plastic bags and frozen to keep them fresh. I am currently working on the packaging which is yet another area in which your influence is very evident: Each bag of peas bears a large photo of you. Thanks to sophisticated computer software, you appear eagerly to be tucking into a large bowl of peas. There is also a large caption reading: 'Henby Peas: The Major force in vegetables'. A speech bubble also proclaims: 'John Major knows, you are what you eat!'

I hope to expand my business by selling my peas to the supermarkets. Watch this space!

I wonder whether you would like to make a special appearance at my market stall and perhaps take charge of the pea-tasting service. I would be honoured to have you there and I am confident that your presence would boost sales.

Please let me know when you would be free.

Yours truly

Julian Henby

NO RESPONSE

Julian Henby

Flat 12
Burgess Hill
West Sussex

15 February 2007

Mr Barry McGuigan (former boxer)
London

Dear Mr McGuigan

I have a neighbour with a serious attitude problem. He tries to prevent me from using the footpath to my front door, he throws his rubbish into my garden, plays loud music late at night and has heated arguments with his spouse during which they engage in drunken brawls. Recently, he demolished one of my trees (because one of its branches was growing into his garden). In short, he is a real nuisance and my nerves are now shot to pieces.

I have made numerous complaints to the council but to no avail. So, I have decided it's time to confront my neighbour and try to make him see sense. I intend to go round there for a long chat asap. The trouble is, although he is in his sixties he is a very large man with big muscles and tattoos. Frankly, he scares me rather a lot.

That is why I am writing to you. Would you be willing to come with me to see my neighbour? I would certainly not be looking for violence but I feel I might need some protection and he might be less aggressive with someone closer his own size. If you could wear your boxer shorts, gum-shield and gloves I think that would really create the right effect.

When would you be free?

Yours truly

J. Henby

NO RESPONSE

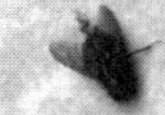

Julian Henby

Flat 12
Burgess Hill
West Sussex

15 January 2007

Ms Carol Vorderman MBE
Bristol

Dear Ms Carol Vorderman

A terrible disease has hit my family and I am writing to you because of your experience in this area. The problem concerns my brother (Dave) who has become terribly addicted to Sudoku. The problem started about one year ago when he got in with 'the wrong crowd' at Brighton railway station. Poor Dave was standing outside WHSmith awaiting his train when he noticed a small group of young people doing Sudoku in the shadows behind the shop. Sadly, curiosity got the better of Dave and he approached the gang for a closer look. Within minutes, Dave had been introduced to his first 'hit' and was on the slippery slope to the living hell of Sudoku addiction.

In the early days, it was just one or two Sudoku hits at the weekend. Then Dave found himself doing it in the evenings too as a means of escape from his problems. Within two months, he needed a hit each morning just to get out of bed and another one after breakfast to get him through the journey to work. Over the past year Dave has become a different person: a stranger. He has lost his zest for life and Sudoku dominates his every waking minute. Last week Dave lost the position he had held at the call centre for seven years, his relationships are at breaking point and his world seems to be falling apart at the seams.

Needless to say, we are all very worried for Dave.

Nothing we do seems to help poor Dave. We have tried to force him to see the damage he is causing himself and to face up to the person he has become but it is as if he is locked away in his own world. On one occasion we even tied Dave's hands behind his back when the craving for Sudoku was upon him, but he somehow managed to get his fix using just his mouth.

I am at my wit's end and I cannot do this on my own anymore, I need help! You have been through this nightmare and recovered so I turn to you for help. How did you do it? Where can I find the light at the end of this horrible tunnel? Please help if you can.

Yours truly

Julian Henby

Julian Henby

ohn Miles Organisation

*Representing The Finest Talent*

January 17th 2007

Julian Henby
Ernest Kleinwort Court
Oakenfield
Burgess Hill
West Sussex RH15 8SJ

Dear Julian

I have passed your letter to Carol and we are sorry to hear of your brother Dave's problems. Maybe he should buy Carol's latest book, "Super Brain – 101 Easy Ways to a More Agile Mind" which has just been published and this may take his mind off Sudoku.

Best wishes

JOHN MILES

PERSONAL MANAGER CAROL VORDERMAN

Flat 12
Burgess Hill
West Sussex

19 January 2007

Mr John Miles
Bristol

Dear John

Many thanks for your letter of 17 January.

Thank you for your suggestion that poor Dave should try reading Carol's book, 'Super Brain – 101 Easy Ways to a More Agile Mind'. However, I fear that it would be unwise to encourage Dave to try yet another method to alter his mind! Who knows where it would lead him? I wouldn't want to be responsible for leading him onto the fast-track road to self-destruction.

I am praying that Ms Vorderman will be able to offer some guidance.

By the way, I am afraid I got rather confused in my previous letter. You see, it is not Sudoku that poor Dave is addicted to but *Sambuka*!

I always get those two muddled up. Sorry about that.

Kind regards.

Yours truly

JH

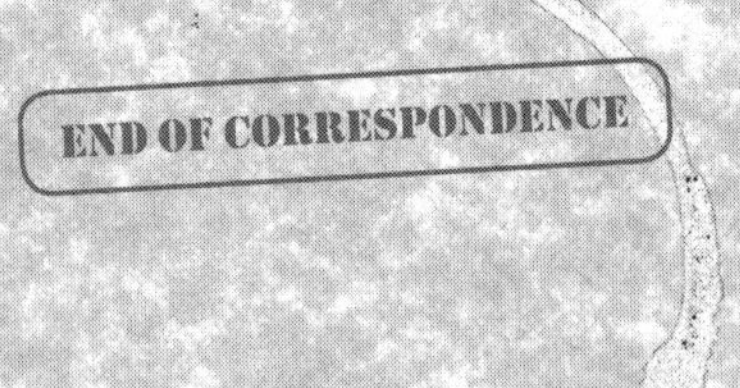


Julian Henby

Flat 12
Burgess Hill
West Sussex

16 February 2007

Tom Baker (TV Actor)
London

Dear Tom

My mother (who is eighty) is convinced that you left a message on her telephone answering machine, asking her out for dinner.

When she told me this, I was initially dubious (Mother frequently gets confused). However, she is adamant that it was your voice (although she admits that you did not leave your name), and she is a very honest person.

Mother recently met a man at her bridge club and they have been having a relationship for several weeks now. However, she is so excited by your message that she is planning to 'let Jim down gently'.

In your message, you did not specify when or where the date should take place. She would be grateful if you would call back soon.

I trust you will treat Mother well. I look forward to welcoming you to the family.

Yours truly

J. Henby

NO RESPONSE

Julian Henby

Flat 12
Burgess Hill
West Sussex

10 December 2006

To: Mr Frank Carson

Dear Frankie

I have been a big fan of your comedy for many years. Hoorah for alcohol-fuelled Irish comedy!

Anyway, I understand that you have been awarded the 'Key To Dublin', allowing you access to every nook and cranny of the great city. I write to you for advice on obtaining the 'Key To Burgess Hill' – my home town! I have a very good reason for wanting such a key: You see, I was involved in an unfortunate incident last month on a visit to my favourite public house. During my visit I became convinced that the barmaid was in fact a man in drag, and it was only when I attempted to prove this to my friends (by the most obvious means) that I realised my mistake. I was then escorted out of the premises by a rather tactile security guard who suffered from various forms of bodily odour (including flatulence). It wasn't until the following day (when I attempted to access a different pub) that I learned that I had been registered on the local 'Pub Watch' scheme and was therefore barred from *all* licensed bars in the area!

Considering this whole thing is the result of a silly misunderstanding, my exclusion from my favourite pubs is obviously unjustified, but try telling that to the local publicans!

Well, dear Frankie, there is only one thing for it: I shall have to obtain the 'Key To Burgess Hill'! That way I could roam the town to my heart's content and if anyone tried to block my entry I would simply let myself in with the magic key! As if brandishing a crucifix at a hoard of blood-thirsty vampires, I would march through my town wielding my key and imbibing of the local ale.

I would be grateful if you would kindly outline the qualifying procedure for obtaining the great key. I pray that it does not involve any demeaning rituals.

Yours truly

Julian Henby

Julian Henby

THANK YOU JULIAN FOR YOUR LETTER IT WAS QUITE FUNNY. I WAS THE MAYOR OF BALBRIGGAN ON 2 OCCASIONS AND IT BORED THE ASS OFF ME. I GAVE A LECTURE TO 130 SCHOOL CHILDREN ON THE ENVIRONMENT AND SPOKE FOR 20 MINUTES ON THE WAY TO WIN THE TIDY TOWN OF IRELAND. I HAD THESE MERE 6-7 AND 8 YEAR OLDS HYPNOTISED BY MY SPARKLING REPARTEE I THEN SAID ANYONE WANT TO ASK ANY QUESTIONS ONE LONE HAND WENT UP - WHAT IS IT? I SAID TO THIS 7 YEAR OLD INTELECTUAL HE REPLIED. "WHEN ARE YOU LEAVING"? MY ADVICE TO YOU JULIAN WOULD BE START AFRESH LEAVE WEST SUSSEX HEAD FOR DUBAI JOIN THE A.A.A.A. THEY DRIVE YA TO DRINK

Thank you for your letter Julian I en- a Photo. There are only 11,000 left.

Frank
Conroy
now at 10
"Sober"

END OF CORRESPONDENCE

Flat 12
Burgess Hill
West Sussex

23 Feb 2007

Mr Jeremy Clarkson
BBC Television Centre
Wood Lane
London, W12 7RJ

Dear Mr Jeremy Clarkson

I am a car enthusiast but I am also a man of science and I know that we cannot continue to produce vehicles that pollute our environment with noxious gases without suffering seriously adverse consequences. For the sake of our health and the health of our planet, we must strive toward finding alternative designs for cars and novel forms of fuel.

In addition to being a researcher in the field of conservation, I am also a semi-professional inventor. Eight years ago I determined to combine these two areas of interest to invent a car that would inflict only a minimum degree of environmental damage. The task soon became something of an obsession. After hundreds of failures, I have at last invented a car that runs on organic matter and produces absolutely no pollution while running! In essence, the car's fuel is identical to food stuffs consumed by humans except that it contains high quantities of fats and sugars.

I am confident that my design has the potential to revolutionise the automobile industry world-wide if only it is given the exposure and backing it deserves. I would be most grateful if you would consider featuring the vehicle on your *Top Gear* television programme.

Please confirm whether you would be willing to become involved in any way.

I am sending you a diagrammatic outline of the vehicle's design (patents pending).

Yours truly

Julian Henby

Julian Henby

# Environmentally Friendly Car With Amazing New Engine Design!

Flat 12
Burgess Hill
West Sussex

15 January 2007

Mr Nicholas Parsons
5th Floor
London

Dear Mr Parsons

I have been having a massive clearout to get rid of all the junk in my flat.

I would like to stage a big garage sale to make a few bob for my troubles and it will be the *Sale Of The Century*! I would be honoured to have you host the event. The plan is to hold auctions and competitions. It looks set to be just like your 80s television show!

If you could employ a couple of glamorous (lady) assistants, that would be great. Also, my brother (Dave) owns a caravan that could be converted into a 'trailer' if required.

When would be most convenient for you?

Yours truly

J. Henby

Julian Henby

# Diamond Management

Jean Diamond ♦ Lesley Duff

31 Percy Street
London
W1T 2DD

Tel: 020 7631 0400
Fax: 020 7631 0500
agents@diman.co.uk
www.diman.co.uk

19th January 2007

Julian Henby
Flat 12

Burgess Hill
West Sussex

Dear Julian Henby

Thank you for your letter regarding Nicholas Parsons. Please let me know the financial offer.

Yours sincerely

**Jean Diamond**

Flat 12
Burgess Hill
West Sussex

23 January 2007

Ms Jean Diamond
Diamond Management
London

Dear Ms Diamond

Many thanks for your letter of 19 January.

I am very pleased that Nicholas Parsons is willing to consider being the host of my massive garage sale. It is sure to be a momentous day!

You asked about my financial offer. I am afraid I am rather poor at present, having recently moved up here to get away from a disastrous life in Cornwall. However, I could auction off one of my brother Dave's frocks (I'll sneak into his wardrobe when he's at the psychiatrist's office) and Mr Parsons would be very welcome to the proceeds of the auction. Would he be prepared to model the dress?

It would be an honour to meet Mr Parsons and I know he would give my garage sale a huge boost.

I look forward to hearing from you soon.

Yours truly

JH

Julian Henby

Flat 12
Burgess Hill
West Sussex

11 March 2007

Mr Des Lynam
London

Dear Mr Lynam

Despite my best efforts I have been single for some time and rarely attract any ladies. This gets frustrating and I feel something must be done before I go mad!

By all accounts, you are something of a 'babe magnet'. On many occasions I have listened to women exalting your good looks and general sexual appeal. You are, then, the ultimate role model for me! Recently, I realised that if only I had your looks and animal magnetism, I too would be getting attractive to women.

With this in mind I am in the process of transforming myself into you! I have studied your preferred attire and will copy it henceforth. My hair-style is identical to yours too and has even been dyed grey. I have grown a moustache (which will be dyed in due course) and I am using makeup to match your skin tone. Only a few short days ago I resembled any other twenty-eight-year-old ginger-haired bloke, but now I am fast becoming the absolute spitting image of you!

The trouble is, there is something missing. I feel I may be lacking some of your charisma and this is something that cannot be emulated with clothing and hair-dos. It seems the only way to obtain this quality is to be mentored by the master himself: Des Lynam!

I do not care how much it costs me – you must teach me all you know about the art of seduction.

When would you be free to discuss your new role?

Yours truly

Julian Henby

Julian Henby

**NO RESPONSE**

Flat 12
Burgess Hill
West Sussex

11 March 2007

Ms Kate Winslet
London

Dear Kate

I am a big fan of yours and believe that I have seen all of your films. One film in particular had a very profound effect on me and has changed the direction of my life. That film is *Titanic*.

Your performance in *Titanic* excited me so much that I ran from the cinema straight home to my computer and logged onto the internet. I could not get the image out of my mind of you standing at the front of the ship, your pose suggesting a beautiful figurehead. Yours surely *is* a face that could launch a thousand ships! I trawled several websites selling various boats, yachts and other vessels. Eventually, I found one that I could afford: a small fishing boat. I had the boat delivered to my home on a trailer and spent several weeks restoring it. It is named Kate after you.

I have given up my job at the office to make a living catching fish. Last week I took *Kate* to Brighton marina for her maiden voyage. During the trip, however, it occurred to me that something was missing: the figurehead in my mental image!

So I contacted a professional woodcarver who agreed to produce a life-sized figurehead for the good ship *Kate*. The trouble is, he is rather a perfectionist and insists on having access to the object (or person) that he is reproducing.

I would be eternally grateful if you would kindly give up some of your time (six hours per day for three weeks) to be my model. This would involve reproducing your *Titanic* pose in my boat while my woodcarver sculpts the figurehead. I would also like to have you installed in the front of the boat while I go for a few fishing trips so I can be confident that the figurehead won't unbalance the boat. And, of course, you will be required to be my substitute figurehead for all voyages until the wooden one is complete. Don't worry, Kate – you will be securely lashed to the boat with ropes.

Please let me know when you would be free to spend the required amount of time with me.

Yours truly

Julian Henby

Flat 12
Burgess Hill
West Sussex

8 July 2007

Baroness Margaret Thatcher
House of Lords
London SW1A 0PW

Dear Lady Thatcher

In my opinion you were one of the greatest Prime Ministers of all time and I applaud you. It is with trepidation that I approach you regarding a matter that you may well (understandably) find ridiculous.

For the past few years I have required regular assistance with everyday housekeeping tasks. The job that I find most difficult is ironing, so two years ago I employed a young Polish lady to do this twice per week. Until recently, everything was going fine and I have always been very happy with her work. However, about three months ago someone in a public house made conversation with her on the subject of politics and referred to you as an 'Iron Lady'.

Since then the stupid girl has become convinced that you (the former leader of our country) was once employed as some kind of cleaner, ironing your employer's shirts! She therefore believes that the position of 'Iron Lady' should be regarded as extremely prestigious and that this has not been properly reflected in her salary!

So my brazen cleaner is threatening to resign unless I double her wages – something I simply *cannot* afford to do. Whenever I try to explain the true meaning of the title 'Iron Lady' she simply accuses me of swindling her out of her rightful remuneration. I would hate to lose her and I really do not feel up to the task of interviewing for new staff these days.

I know this is a terrible imposition but I would be most grateful if you would kindly write a brief statement describing the intended meaning of 'Iron Lady'. I could then show this to my cleaner and straighten out this ridiculous misunderstanding. She *simply will not* listen to anyone else but I am convinced she will take notice of you.

I would very much appreciate your assistance.

Yours truly

Julian Henby

Flat 12
Burgess Hill
West Sussex

15 January 2007

Mr Gary Lineker
c/o BBC Broadcasting House
Portland Place
London, W1A 1AA

Dear Mr Lineker

Hopefully you will recall being involved in the production and marketing of a brand of crisps the flavour of which was 'Salt & Lineker'.

Some time ago I consumed a bag of your 'Salt & Lineker' flavoured crisps from a reputable retailer. At the time of consumption I found the crisps most flavoursome and delightfully crisp. After finishing my packet of crisps I allowed their memory to recede to the back of my mind... until very recently.

Last weekend I was enjoying a game of cards with a group of associates when the subject of 'leisure eating' crept into the conversation. Somehow the focus of our debate became your crisps. One of my fellow card players explained that the 'Salt & Lineker' brand had been withdrawn from the market because the 'Lineker' element of the crisps was in fact harvested from Gary Lineker's own body! Knowing that I had consumed a bag of these crisps some years earlier, I was naturally appalled to learn this fact (please do not take offence, Gary – it's just that I am more used to consuming *animal* products).

Please would you let me know exactly which part of your body was used in the production of your crisps and whether it could have damaged me in any way.

I anxiously await your reply.

Yours truly

Julian Henby

Julian Henby

# GARY LINEKER

1 February, 2007

Mr. Julian Henby,
Flat 12,

Burgess Hill,
West Sussex

Dear Mr. Henby,

Thank you for your letter of 15 January.

Rest assured you are completely safe – and my sense of humour remains intact!

Kind regards

Yours sincerely,

GARY LINEKER

END OF CORRESPONDENCE

Flat 12
Burgess Hill
West Sussex

15 February 2007

Ms JK Rowling
London

Dear Ms Rowling

I have been reading your wonderful *Harry Potter* books to my brother Dave for some time and he is now Harry Potter mad!

In fact, he is so captivated by your books that he insists on being called Harry Potter (which is not his real name). He has also taken to wearing a wizard's cape and a pair of my old spectacles. This fantasy of his is probably harmless (unlike his obsession with Jimmy Savile). However, there has been an unfortunate consequence for my young niece.

You see, my brother has been 'casting spells' on my niece to make her bark like a dog and suchlike. She is probably old enough not to take her uncle's witchcraft too seriously on the whole. However, my brother recently cast a spell to turn her into a frog!

This only became a problem when she developed a slight cold and her mother commented on the 'frog in her throat'. Since this comment was made, my niece has become convinced that the various symptoms of her virus are in fact the hallmarks of her metamorphosis into a frog! Her mother and I assumed that these fears would be forgotten very quickly, but my niece only grows more anxious as time goes by (even though her cold is gone). We have tried many approaches to put her mind at rest but to no avail, and I am now rather concerned.

I wonder whether you might be kind enough to formulate a special spell for my niece to reverse the one cast by my brother. My hope is that any 'spell' coming directly from you will be more powerful than anything we (mere muggles) could manage.

Many thanks.

Yours truly

Julian Henby

Julian Henby

Flat 12
Burgess Hill
West Sussex

11 March 2007

Mr Joe Pasquale
High Holborn
London

Dear Mr Pasquale

I have seen you on television many times and enjoy your comic performances. Although I did not see it, I am told that you once partook in a feast of insects in the jungle while making a TV show. I am also told that you rather enjoyed your meal!

Three years ago I qualified as a chef and even opened my own restaurant. Unfortunately, a freak accident with a food blender forced me to give up my career, but I am still passionate about food. I have been ostracised from the catering industry because of my unusual choice of cooking ingredients which include cockroaches, flies, maggots, spiders, moths, woodlice and many other insects. However, I am not prepared to be influenced by my small-minded critics because I firmly believe that the world of insects represents a rich source of food. It is a category that has been totally neglected in the Western world for too long.

My mission is to promote the use of insects in food. I have therefore written a book of 100 insect recipes ranging from centipede salads to wasp pizzas. I have found most publishers to be rather negative about my book so I am publishing it privately.

I feel my mission would receive a huge boost if a popular celebrity like you were associated with it, so I am planning a celebrity event to raise money for charity (and also to promote my book). The event is called *The Big Insect Feast* and will require 10 celebrities to eat nothing but insect recipes for a period of one month. During this time they will each keep personal diaries, extracts of which will be printed in the book! I would be deeply honoured if you would kindly volunteer for the project. All proceeds will go toward helping people in the Third World (where insect food sources are well utilised).

Please let me know whether you would be prepared to get involved.

Yours truly

NO RESPONSE

JH

Julian Henby

Flat 12
Burgess Hill
West Sussex

30 January 2007

Mr James Herbert
Golden Square

Dear Mr Herbert

My mother (who is nearly 80) insists that your books are the work of Satan. This wouldn't be a problem except that I recently split up with my fiancée (Rebecca) and now live with my mother. Mother tries to prevent me from reading your books and intercepts any that I bring into the house.

The other day I tried to smuggle in one of your novels. I hid it inside a box of *Cheerio's* but she carried out her usual thorough search and discovered the book, screaming '*Devil worshipper!*' After incinerating the book in the garden, Mother made me burn my clothes before getting into a bath of near-scolding water to have my skin scrubbed with a wire brush to cleanse me of evil. I had to take the following day off work and when I did return to my job I nearly got fired because my boss thought I had taken a trip abroad where I had received severe sunburn. In reality, my skin had become pink from all that scrubbing.

If I get caught actually reading your books I have to be cleansed from the *inside*. God knows you don't want to know about that!

It is clear there is only one way to convince Mother that your books are harmless and won't condemn me to Hell: she will have to meet you! Would you be willing to come to our home and see her? It is imperative that you wear something non-scary and perhaps a crucifix. Mother approves of a suit and tie but the jacket must be worn and the tie should match your socks. If you also carried a bible I think it would put her at ease.

If Mother gets it into her head that you are Satan and becomes too agitated, there is a chance she might attempt to set light to you. But don't be unduly concerned: I will be ready with a bucket of water.

Please let me know when you could come and see Mother. We really do need to get all of this sorted out.

Yours truly

Julian Henby

Julian Henby

13th February 2007.

Dear Ernest,

How did your mother know? In public (mainly in daylight) I've managed to pose as a perfectly normal human, but she must have seen something in my work (or possibly my book jackets) that has obviously made her suspicious.

I do admire how she wire-scrubs your naked flesh with near-scalding water (but why only <u>near</u>-scalding?). I'm disappointed that you didn't describe how she cleanses you from the <u>inside</u> though; that sounds very appealing.

Unfortunately, I only make personal calls when people are sleeping: it's so easy to slip into their nightmares. But I do know the region of Burgess Hill quite well – it's so like a graveyard in the dark hours. I enjoy peering through half-drawn curtains, especially on the upper floors. People are amusing when they think they're unwatched.

Thank you for letting me know your mother's address. Tell her to expect me.

In anticipation.

James Herbert

Flat 12
Burgess Hill
West Sussex

15 February 2007

Mr James Herbert
Golden Square
London

Dear Mr Herbert

Thank you for your letter of 13 February. Number 13 – unlucky for some, and God knows I can believe that now!

This communication will be kept short because it is so exhausting to type with my mouth. Besides, Mother will be back shortly.

I made the mistake of neglecting properly to hide your letter from Mother. Unfortunately, she discovered it during a routine search of my bedroom. Upon reading it, she let out a terrible scream – a sound I had never heard Mother emit before and I pray never to again! With hands contorted into trembling talons, she fell to her knees and wailed in agony as if the words before her were written, not in ink, but in flesh-eating acid. She turned to me in disbelief, her face screaming, '*Why! Why!*', but her expression quickly softened, morphing into compassion. Perhaps maternal instinct was more powerful than fear – I like to think this was what directed her next actions.

Mother sprang to work, ushering me toward the bathroom. Between shallow breaths she explained that your letter was an interface between worlds: Satan had entered my body when fingertips pressed against paper. He would soon travel through the flesh towards my soul, but there was still time. So far, only my hands were infested with evil. Turning the cable of an electric toothbrush into a tourniquet, Mother set about isolating the evil in my left arm. She was sure it had not yet reached the upper arm but she tied the cable high to be sure. Then she bound my other arm.

When she left the room, I had time to worry about what her plan was, but not much time. Mother soon returned with the axe and was mercifully swift with it.

I don't remember much after that, James. I must go now: Mother is worried that the words in your letter acted as couriers of evil, infecting my eyes. I can hear her rifling through cutlery in the kitchen, selecting her tool.

Goodbye, James

JH

Julian Henby

**END OF CORRESPONDENCE**

Flat 12
Burgess Hill
West Sussex

21 February 2007

Sir Anthony Hopkins
Warrington

Dear Sir Anthony Hopkins

I am a big fan of your films, particularly your earlier work. However, I am writing to you regarding a personal matter.

Like a fool, I recently allowed my six-year-old nephew to watch *Silence of the Lambs* on video when he was staying with me for a few days. His mother (my sister) informs me that he has been refusing to eat meat of any kind since his visit. Apparently, he is worried that a human organ may have found its way into his steak and kidney pie. Clearly, my nephew's fears could only have been triggered by the unusual dietary requirements of Hannibal Lecter in your film. However, my nephew obviously has not yet reported my error to his mother and I am not about to spill the beans! A saucepan has been known to become a deadly weapon in the hands of my sister, so I must keep my silence for the sake of my health.

I imagine you carried out extensive research for *Silence of the Lambs*. Perhaps you even met tribes or individuals that consume human meat. If so, would you be kind enough to send me details of how I might contact such people? If my nephew were introduced to people who choose this lifestyle perhaps he would forget his fear and go back to his favourite meat pies.

I would be most grateful for any help you can offer. We are all suffering badly from this difficult situation.

Yours truly

Julian Henby

NO RESPONSE

Julian Henby

Flat 12
Burgess Hill
West Sussex

21 February 2007

Master Beefeater
The Tower of London
Tower Hill
Greater London EC3N 4AB

Dear Sir

I believe you employ a team of guards known as the Beefeaters who protect the Queen from deranged vegetarians who might attempt to invade the Tower. I have been told that these guards routinely appear at the windows of the Tower of London, devouring raw steaks of beef in a show of superiority and power. Apparently, any vegetarians approaching the Tower are repelled by the guards who tear chunks off their steaks and hurl them at the animal-sympathisers below.

I am a vegetarian and I must say that I take offence at these unseemly displays by your Beefeaters. I have no intention of storming the Tower. Nor do I know of any other vegetarians who are planning to invade.

How can you defend this kind of unnecessary taunting behaviour?

I look forward to hearing from you soon.

Yours truly

JH

Julian Henby

Historic Royal Palaces is the independent charity that looks after the Tower of London, Hampton Court Palace, the Banqueting House, Kensington Palace and Kew Palace. We help everyone explore the story of how monarchs and people have shaped society, in some of the greatest palaces ever built.

We receive no funding from the Government or the Crown, so we depend on the support of our visitors, members, donors, volunteers and sponsors.

28 February 2007

Mr Julian Henby
Flat 12

Burgess Hill
West Sussex

Dear Mr Henby

Thank you for your letters to both our Chief Yeoman Warder and General Manager recently.

I am unsure where you have picked up these rumours, but they are completely unfounded. Some of our Yeoman Warders are actually vegetarians themselves! The term 'beefeater' most likely comes from the fact that Yeoman Warders were at one time paid their salary in beef. This was a very long time ago, however the name has stuck.

I trust that this helps put your mind at rest – if not, why don't you come to visit the Tower sometime and see for yourself? I've enclosed some visitor information with this letter showing our opening time, prices etc.

Yours sincerely

Claire Ashford
Visitor Services Manager

Flat 12
Burgess Hill
West Sussex

10 March 2007

Ms Claire Ashford
Visitor Services Manager
HM Tower of London
London EC3N 4AB

Dear Claire

Many thanks for your letter of 28 February assuring me that your Beefeaters do not, in fact, taunt visiting vegetarians with raw steaks of beef.

My brother Dave is the swine who spun me this yarn about your Yeomen. It seems that he was just trying to terrify me with this horror story so that I would choose to sleep with our bedroom light switched on. You see, he likes to rearrange his theatrical costumes late at night with the lights on and this is a constant source of friction between us. Understandably, I prefer to turn off the lights at 11.30 to go to sleep. The mere knowledge that Dave has donned one of his bally frocks in the dark to practice his routine is invariably bad enough without actually seeing him!

To wreak my revenge on Dave, I have hidden his favourite brassiere (the one that doesn't chafe). I plan to tell him that the parrot ate it.

Anyway, many thanks for inviting me to visit the Tower. Unfortunately, I must decline the offer because of a debilitating phobia. However, I showed the information to my mother (she is eighty). She is very keen to take the tour and has asked me to enquire about access for the disabled.

I look forward to hearing from you.

Yours truly

END OF CORRESPONDENCE

JH

Julian Henby

Flat 12
Burgess Hill
West Sussex

11 March 2007

Sir Paul McCartney
London

Dear Sir Paul

Since the 1960s I have been a big fan of your pop group *The Beatles*. In addition to listening to music, I also try to do my bit for charity and I have been working on a new campaign.

My plan is to combine my great respect for your music with my desire to help those in need. Last month I ventured into my aunt's overgrown garden in search of beetles – not Ringo, George, Paul and John but the insects! Several hours later, I emerged from the jungle with four large beetles safely confined to a margarine pot. The next fourteen days were spent on the delicate task of crafting a set of miniature musical instruments from thin wire: guitars; piano; cello; and drums. The tiny sculptures featured intricate details that could be appreciated only with the use of a magnifying glass. Using tiny drops of superglue, I fastened my miniature instruments to the limbs of their respective musicians who were named after the members of your group. Paul was on lead guitar, Ringo on drums, John on piano, and finally George on the cello. At last, my band was born. I called it *The Little Beetles*.

Using a cardboard crate, I fashioned a stage for *The Little Beetles* which I placed upon a large stereo speaker. With my band of beetles nicely arranged on their stage, I pressed *Play* on my CD machine. A moment later *She Loves You, Yeah, Yeah, Yeah!* was blasting from the speaker and the cardboard stage was vibrating in beat with the music. It was at this point that a wonderful thing happened: *The Little Beetles* started to move, miming the song with their instruments, their small legs dancing to the rhythm! It truly was a miracle!

I am making it my mission to tour the country with my band, performing concerts at every old people's home and hospital in the UK. At the end of the show, I collect money for charity but the concerts are technically free.

I would be honoured to have you involved with the promotion of my band. Would you be prepared to kick-start our publicity campaign by coming to one of our shows and speaking to the media?

I look forward to hearing from you.

Yours truly

Julian Henby

Julian Henby

Flat 12
Burgess Hill
West Sussex

22 February 2007

Mr Peter Duncan, Chief Scout
The Scouts Association
London

Dear Mr Duncan

Firstly, let me say that I consider you to be the greatest *Blue Peter* presenter of all time and I feel honoured to be in contact with you.

As a boy, I was a member of the Scouts and I have many fond memories of those days. In addition to being fun, the Scouts educated me in the ways of survival and fostered my self-confidence.

My youngest, Tony is approaching the age at which he will be eligible to join the Scouts and I am very keen for him to do so. I have described to him the many trips and activities that I enjoyed as a lad in the Scouts, and he is very eager to join. Tony enjoys going on long walks in the country and he has a lot of energy so I am sure he will fit in very well. He is also very sociable and loves meeting new friends.

Before I commit to enrolling Tony in the Scouts I need to obtain further details. The thing is that Tony has a number of special requirements as I will now explain: Whilst being unusually small, Tony is also rather stocky and will therefore probably not fit into a standard issue uniform. I wonder whether there is any way to have a uniform specially tailored to fit him. The second issue is Tony's diet that has been scientifically formulated and contains a high level of protein (which he normally gets from processed meats). The final issue has to do with communication: Tony often has difficulty communicating with people and sometimes also fails to understand what people say (even simple instructions).

It is because of these special considerations that I decided to go straight to the top and contact you. Please would you confirm whether your organisation is able to accommodate Tony's unique idiosyncrasies and welcome him into the movement?

I look forward to hearing from you soon.

Yours truly

Julian Henby

Julian Henby

**West Sussex Scouts**

Goring by Sea
West Sussex

Mr Julian Henby
Flat 12,

Burgess Hill
West Sussex

Dear Mr Henby,

Your letter has been forwarded to me as Assistant County Commissioner for Diversity. As you have heard, in Scouting we endeavour to include everyone regardless of special needs and I am keen to do all I can to help with your son. I feel the best way forward would be for us to meet to discuss the matter. This will give me a clearer picture of your sons needs and help us to see if there is a local scout group able to accommodate him.

Yours faithfully

J. M. Greenyer (Mrs)

Jeanne Greenyer ACC Diversity.

Flat 12
Burgess Hill
West Sussex

22 March 2007

Ms Jeanne Greenyer ACC Diversity
West Sussex Scouts
Goring By Sea
West Sussex

Dear Ms Greenyer

Many thanks for your recent letter regarding Tony's special requirements. I must say I am very heartened by your policy of inclusion in the Scouts. In your letter you refer to Tony as my son. However, this is not strictly true although I suppose I am an adoptive parent of sorts (his real father was something of a stray and his mother died some years ago from a gastric torsion).

I would be most grateful if you would answer a few specific questions:

1) Tony's ears are rather protruding, so would it be acceptable if I were to cut two holes in his Scout hat to accommodate them?

2) Would Tony be required to climb any trees in the Scouts? If so, this could be a problem because he seems unable to do so.

3) Would Tony be allowed to bring his favourite tennis ball to Scouts? He hardly goes anywhere without it!

I look forward to hearing from you.

Yours truly

JH

Julian Henby

Goring by Sea
West Sussex

Mr Julian Henby
Flat 12,

Burgess Hill
West Sussex

Dear Mr Henby,
Thank you for your letter. I am sorry I have not replied earlier but like you I have been busy and have also been away.
In answer to your queries the Scouts no longer wear hats as uniform, climbing trees is not an activity the scouts do often so would not cause any problems and I am sure it would not be a problem for Tony to take his tennis ball with him.
I look forward to hearing from you soon to set up a meeting.
I will be away on holiday at the end of the month.

Yours truly

J. M. Greenyer.

Jeanne Greenyer (Mrs)

Flat 12
Burgess Hill
West Sussex

18 April 2007

Mrs Jeanne Greenyer ACC Diversity
West Sussex Scouts
Goring By Sea
West Sussex

Dear Mrs Greenyer

Many thanks for your latest letter via which you answered my most pressing questions.

Little Tony seemed very relieved when I told him that he would be allowed to take his tennis ball to Scouts. Indeed, as a token of his appreciation we are enclosing a drawing of Tony. Tony sat for the portrait last Christmas and he has treasured it ever since.

Kind regards

JH

Julian Henby
(and Tony)

# TONY HENBY - CHRISTMAS 2006

21 May 2007

Flat 12
Burgess Hill
West Sussex

Ms June Brown
'EastEnders'
BBC Elstree Centre
Herts WD6 1JF

Dear June

Ever since the first episode I have been a big fan of *Eastenders* and your character Dot Cotton has remained a firm favourite of mine ever since she first lit up a cigarette and quoted the *New Testament* in that distinctive lecherous voice!

In recent years I have become acutely aware of the terrible damage being wreaked by nicotine addiction in this country. In fact, the numbers of smoking-related deaths have become such a concern that I have made it my mission to stub out this problem in any way I can.

Many smokers take their first cigarette as school children. Therefore, I have decided to focus my energy on bringing the message to these vulnerable young people via their schools. With thirty years experience in the electronics industry, I have drawn on my expertise to create a hi-tech toy with a serious purpose. After two years design and development, I created *Junky The Dragon*. Standing 45cm tall and 165cm long, *Junky* is a highly sophisticated robotic dragon with advanced artificial intelligence. I have enclosed a drawing for you to see. It can move and interact with people entirely independently, allowing it to form real relationships with young children. It can even learn from its mistakes!

I will tour the country visiting schools with *Junky*, hoping that children will be 'blown away' by the spectacle of my dragon scuttling into their classrooms of its own volition. After introducing itself to its young hosts, it will engage them in an honest debate, answering questions on smoking. Due to a rather overdeveloped (and potentially lethal) fire-breathing mechanism, *Junky*'s tour has been delayed one month for modifications. However, I am confident that he will be ready by the autumn. There is, though, one feature that is sadly lacking: *Junky*'s voice!

I trust you will agree that *Junky*'s mission is a worthwhile one, and I hereby invite you to become the voice of *Junky The Dragon*. This would involve recording each of the 10,000 words in *Junky*'s vocabulary so that they can be fed into his super-powerful microprocessor. All necessary recording equipment will be provided.

I do hope you are able to get involved with my campaign.

Yours truly

NO RESPONSE

Julian Henby

Julian Henby

# Junky The Dragon

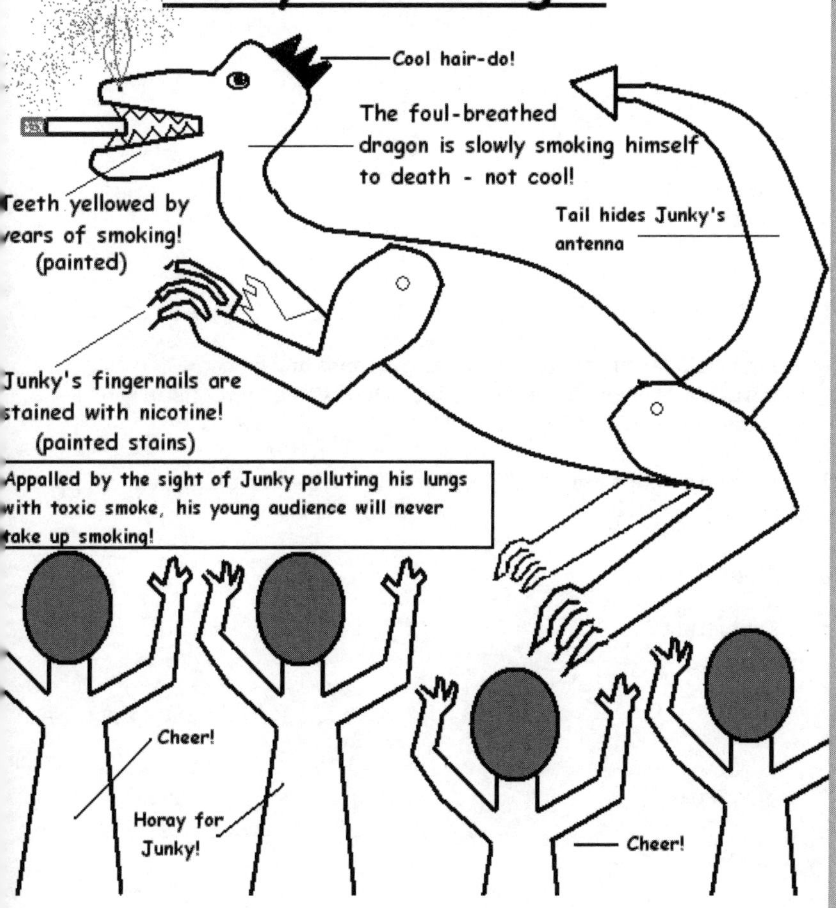

Flat 12
Burgess Hill
West Sussex

11 March 2007

Mr Brian Connolly
Antrim

Dear Brian

I am a big fan of your television programmes and comedy. I particularly enjoyed the TV show in which you toured Australia on a three-wheeled motorcycle.

I would be most grateful if you would kindly send me a signed photograph.

Many thanks.

Yours truly

Julian Henby

Julian Henby

DEAR JULIAN
I DO NOT THINK
YOU HAVE CONTACTED
THIS RIGHT
PERSON
BUT HERE

**brian connolly**

**"Initiate"**

performance 17.00 - 18.00
Sat. 2nd March 2002

installation exhibition
Sat/Sun 3rd - 24th March
14.00 - 18.00
[view by appointment]

***trace:***
installaction artspace

IS MY PHOTO
+ SIGNATURE ANYWAY!
TA BILLY CONNOLLY!
(OR BRIAN CONNOLLY?)

Flat 12
Burgess Hill
West Sussex

18 March 2007

Mr Brian Connolly
Antrim

Dear Brian

I am terribly sorry about the mix up. You must be utterly fed up with people getting you confused with the bearded Scot. I suspect that few people understand the anguish that this sort of confusion can cause. However, I hope you will now take heart in the knowledge that you have at least one kindred spirit: me. I know the pain very well, for there is a young man living in the same road as me with the same name – Julian. But we are two different people, damn it! I demand the right to be a distinct individual!

Yours truly

JH

Julian Henby

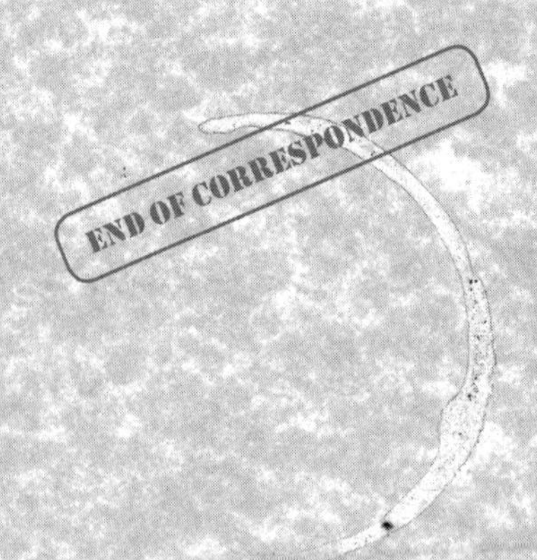

Flat 12
Burgess Hill
West Sussex

8 July 2007

Mr Michael Buerk
London

Dear Mr Buerk

I am a film-maker specialising in documentaries. Inspired by your excellent television series, *999* about real-life rescues and emergencies, I am planning a one-off film called *666*. In this documentary I shall invite a group of mediums and detectives to come together for a séance. Their goal will be to contact the souls of those unfortunate people who have died at the hands of murderers! What's more, they will all be the victims of *unsolved* murders! Using information obtained during the séance from the deceased victims themselves the detectives will follow new leads, piece together new evidence and solve the crimes!

I would be honoured to have you as the presenter for the show. I am already in talks with a major television network and there is every chance of a deal being struck soon. I am prepared to pay a fee that reflects your illustrious track record.

Please confirm whether you are interested.

Yours truly

NO RESPONSE

J. Henby

Julian Henby

Flat 12
Burgess Hill
West Sussex

8 July 2007

Mr Ian Hislop
c/o Private Eye
6 Carlisle Street
London W1D 3BN

Dear Ian

I believe we have a mutual friend in Mr Paul Merton.

Anyway, I am planning a surprise birthday party for Pauly so I am contacting all his old friends in the hope that they will agree to attend. The arrangements for the party have yet to be made but I imagine we will hire a function room and garden for the event.

Please do let me know whether you would like to attend. I hope to have more details for you quite soon.

Remember, Ian: mum's the word!

I look forward to hear from you soon.

Yours truly

Julian Henby

Julian Henby

NO RESPONSE

Flat 12
Burgess Hill
West Sussex

8 July 2007

Mr Gareth Gates
London

Dear Mr Gates

I am a big fan of your music and your success has been a powerful inspiration for me. My greatest ambition is to be a chart-topping singer like you. However, I feel I am being held back because I suffer from a stammer (as you once did). I know you understand very well how frustrating this can be.

Despite my stuttering I am determined to succeed. I have seen many specialists for treatment over the years but nothing can cure me of the affliction (apparently mine is a rare and very severe form of stammer) so I am now resigned to *incorporating* my stuttering somehow into my work. You are probably familiar with records from the 1980s such as 'The Stutter Rap' and '19' that use stuttering to good effect. My mission is to revive this style of music, creating an opportunity for other stammering singers and myself in the industry.

I feel that stammering should officially be seen as a disability within the music world: after all, it can cripple a singer as surely as any other impediment. If stammering were to be classified as a disability, record producers might be more receptive to the types of records designed to utilise the stutter. I am therefore starting a campaign to put the issue of stammering firmly on the agenda at the highest levels of the industry.

Having suffered with a stammer yourself, I know you will sympathise with my plight. I would be honoured to have you involved with the campaign. I am sure your support would propel it into the spotlight.

Please let me know whether you are willing to support my campaign. I will then send you an information pack. I would also be grateful for your expert advice.

Yours truly

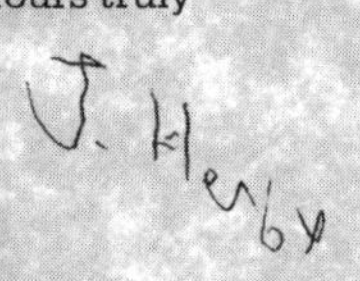

Julian Henby

Flat 12
Burgess Hill
West Sussex

8 July 2007

Sir Steve Redgrave
Steve Redgrave Trust
Hampshire

Dear Sir Steve Redgrave

I am a great admirer of your brilliant career as an Olympic rower. Indeed, your amazing performances on the water even inspired me to purchase a rowing machine for my home and I now boast quite a well-toned body! You can take full credit for this, Steve, and also for the frequent requests by young ladies for permission to run their fingers over my rippling six-pack!

Anyway, in addition to being something of a fitness fanatic (thanks to you) I have been a semi-professional inventor for some years. Although I enjoy keeping myself fit there is no escaping the fact that using a rowing machine can become rather tedious – no match for the thrill of skimming along the water with the wind rushing through one's hair! To rectify this I have invented a revolutionary rowing machine designed to replicate (as far as possible) all the sensations inherent in *real* rowing. In many respects my rower is like any other rowing machine. However, at its base there are two large floats running along the machine's length. These floats provide buoyancy, allowing the machine to float in a well-filled bath where it is intended to be used. At the front of the rower is mounted a fan, connected to the 'oars' by a system of gears. The faster the user rows, the faster the fan spins thus realistically recreating the wind experienced during real rowing. The combination of this wind effect and the sensation of the machine bobbing or listing in the water creates a very authentic rowing experience and eliminates all boredom!

The rowing machine is to be called *The Steve Redgrave Virtual Rower* (I trust you approve) and I have been in talks with a major manufacturer who I hope will get it into the shops by next year. We are planning a big promotional programme touring the country, and it would be wonderful to have you onboard. Would you be prepared to come on the tour and demonstrate the machine? I have enclosed some information (in pictorial form) on this revolutionary design.

Yours truly

J. Henby

Julian Henby

# The Steve Redgrave Rower

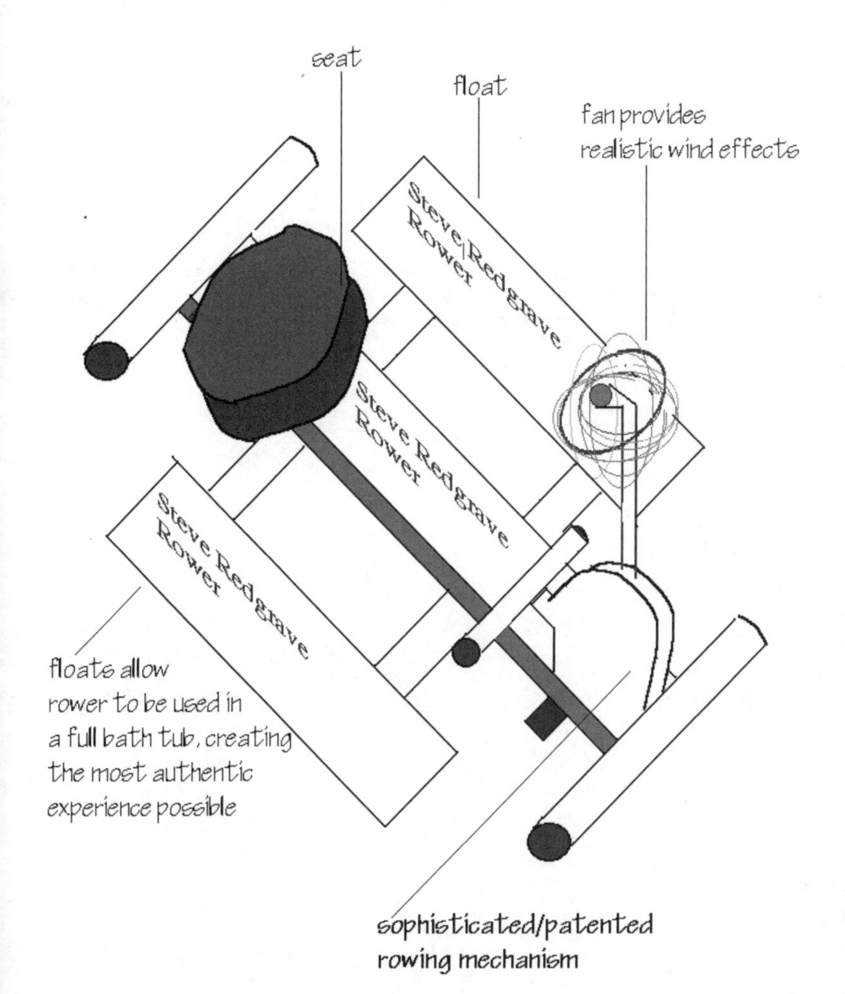

Julian Henby
Flat 12

Burgess Hill
West Sussex

20th August 2007

Dear Julian,

Thank you for your letter and enclosing the details of the planned virtual rower. I am afraid, however, that at this time Sir Steve would not like to be in any way associated with this project. We wish you luck with the development of the Virtual Rower.

Kind regards,

**Michael Pask**
Senior Vice President

Flat 12
Burgess Hill
West Sussex

21 May 2007

Mr Jools Holland, Patron
Deptford
London SE8

Dear Mr Holland

I have heard many great things about you and have no doubt that you are a very talented man. One of the things I have been told is that you have your own 'big band'.

Due to crippling obesity, I have been unable to work for several years. Last year, as a means of relieving my boredom, I decided to set up my own 'big band'. So I embarked on a lengthy search for band members, and I am proud to announce that I now have my band.

Keith was my first recruit: weighing 32 stone, he plays lead guitar. Three weeks later I discovered Ricky J who uses the entirety of his 29 stone frame to pound out a rhythm on drums. Then there's Harvey (34 stone) on bass: the sight of him caressing his bass guitar as it nestles snugly between rolls of fat in his lap is enough to bring a tear to the eye. Finally, I front the band playing keyboards and performing vocals (a good set of lungs lie within my 27 stone body!)

With a combined weight of 122 stone my 'big band' is big indeed but we would like to grow even bigger before applying to Guiness for the world record. Yours is the original 'big band' and I have no doubt that it would rival any band in terms of size (including my own). We would be honoured if you would kindly invite us to merge with your band to become a 'super big band'. This would only be while our application to Guiness is being processed.

Please confirm whether you would be interested in the merger.

Yours truly

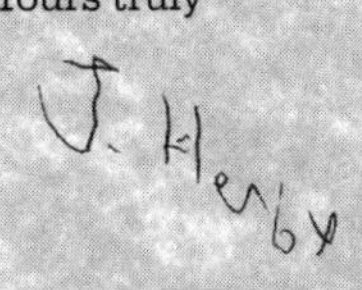

Julian Henby

Flat 12
Burgess Hill
West Sussex

8 July 2007

Michael Fish
London

Dear Mr Fish

I consider you to be the 'Big Daddy' of the weather forecasting world and I applaud you for your unwavering services to metrology (although you cannot hear it I have just given you a round of applause).

Your excellent performance as a weather forecaster never fails to inspire me and it seems my enthusiasm has even rubbed off on my puppy dog, Tony. Not long ago I was preparing for a holiday in north Wales. Everything was packed so I fastened Tony's lead ready to escort him to the car for the trip. However, Tony sat on the doormat, refusing to go. Eventually, I lured him out with a piece of ham and bundled him into the car. Later that day as we neared our destination it became apparent that Tony's reluctance to visit Wales had been well founded. The heavens opened and torrential rain made driving conditions treacherous, forcing us to park in a lay-by until the weather improved. Sitting in the car with rain pounding the metal roof, I looked at Tony in awe of his amazing premonition. Clearly, he possessed some 'sixth sense' that had alerted him to the coming storm! Upon our return to Sussex I set about nurturing Tony's extraordinary talent. I took four $1m^2$ sheets of cupboard and drew a different symbol on each: a rain cloud; a bright sun; a symbol for wind; and one for snow. The symbols were arranged in a row on my lawn and Tony was familiarised with each one. With a mandate to predict the weather for the following day, he was instructed to sit upon the appropriate symbol. The training process took several days because Tony struggled to interpret the abstract symbols. However, once he had mastered this his forecasts proved incredibly accurate: he was achieving up to 70% accuracy!

Computers, of course, have a habit of crashing at the most inopportune moments. I therefore believe that dogs like Tony should be employed by the Met. Office as a backup system. Although Tony's special talent must be terribly rare there probably exists at least one psychic dog living in each region of the UK. If all such dogs were utilised then a useful set of forecasts for the whole country would emerge to substitute (or complement) those produced by your supercomputers.

May I bring Tony to the Met. Office for a meeting with you and your colleagues? We could discuss how to take this to the next level. I have also contacted various television/radio networks because I feel my discovery is of public interest – it's a huge story! I trust you would not object to me saying that I am working in association with you – this should add to my credibility.

Please let me know when Tony and I can visit. I have enclosed a drawing of Tony to show his enthusiasm at the prospect.

Yours truly

Julian Henby

Julian Henby

# Tony The Dog Forecasts The Weather

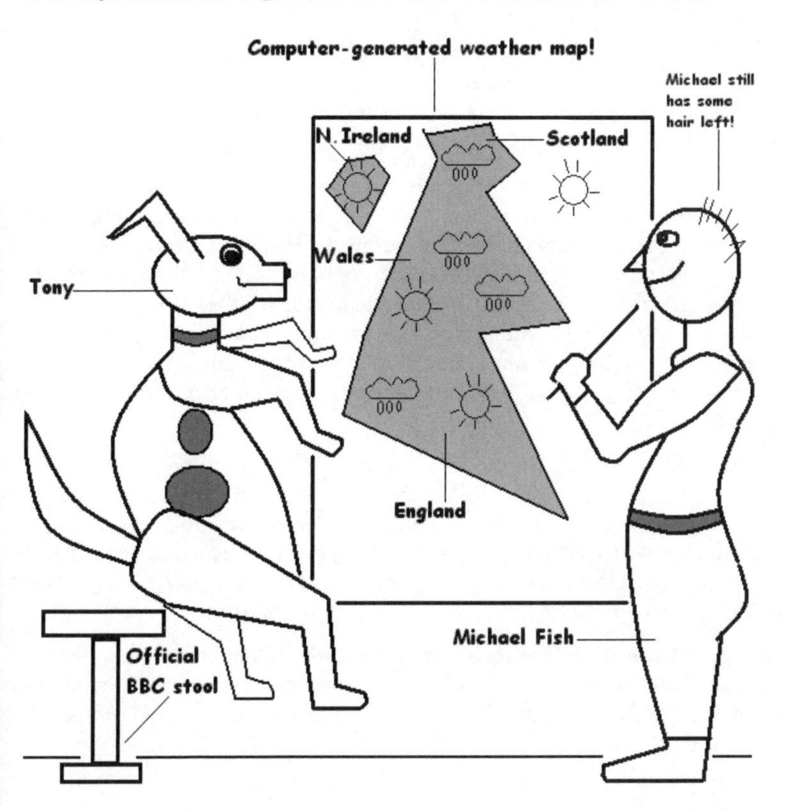

Flat 12
Burgess Hill
West Sussex

11 March 2007

Mr Matthew Kelly, President
Cheshire

Dear Matthew

I am a fan of your television show *Stars In Their Eyes* in which contestants dress up like their favourite singers to perform renditions of hit songs.

My mother (who is eighty) is now too infirm to live alone so she recently moved into my flat. She has been retired for some time and therefore doesn't contribute much money toward my expenses. However, I watched a television programme a few weeks ago about old-style travelling circuses, and this gave me an idea. You see, for the past few years Mother has sported a little white beard (much like the goatees favoured by young men), so my idea is to find her employment as a 'Bearded Lady' in a travelling show! This would enable Mother to pay her way and also give us both some time alone.

The trouble is I have been in contact with several travelling shows and circuses but none has had a vacancy for a 'Bearded Lady'. The TV programme suggested that such performers were once very popular, but perhaps there is less call for them these days (probably thanks to the Xbox). I seem to have tried every potential employer I can imagine and I am now out of ideas. I am therefore turning to you for assistance.

As an experienced presenter of a successful TV talent show, you must be an expert on the entertainment industry. Please would you be kind enough to advise me on how best to find Mother a job. I would be most grateful for your help.

If the 'Bearded Lady' idea turns out to be a dead-end I also have another idea: exotic dancer to the male clientele of an old people's home (provided her pads are sufficiently reliable).

I look forward to hearing from you.

Yours truly

Julian Henby

Julian Henby

personal stationery exclusively designed at NMC Trading Limited - a charity serving individuals with muscular dystrophy.

Julian Henby,
Flat 12,

BURGESS HILL,
West Sussex

10th April 2007.

Dear Julian,

Thanks so much for you letter and glad to hear that you enjoyed 'Stars In Their Eyes' – I enjoyed doing the show so much but am also thrilled to have moved on and concentrate on tv and theatre drama.

Thank you too for asking my advice on how to break your mother into the world of show business. A very tough and brave choice for her, and you, to make. It is, as you are discovering, not an easy career path to take. But knock backs are to be expected and are not, I am sure, a personal reflection on your mother or indeed the way you are approaching potential employers – it is just that competition is so fierce.

The field that you feel your mother fits into is a very narrow and old-fashioned one indeed, and here perhaps lies your problem. As one who has for years perused the pages of The Stage and Television Today, it has not escaped my notice that some of the more exotic job opportunities are becoming very thin on the ground as creativity and initiative are replaced by the need to pander to the masses. Together with the falling numbers of circus troupes and touring vaudeville, and the new fangled emphasis on individuals' rights and human dignity mean often that what used to be looked on as entertainment is now frowned upon instead.

Sadly, your alternative idea throws up a wealth of Health and Safety pitfalls for the carers of those approaching the end of their rainbows. Much as many of those clientele you mention would appreciate, delight even, in your mother's performances, the heightened risk of coronaries amongst her audience and the possible ensuing litigation must give pause to most, if not all, potential employers.

I can only suggest that you ask your mother if she has any other hidden skills that you might be able to exploit or conversely perhaps she could become the home-maker and you could explore the delights of the job centre. Of course, there is always X Factor.

Good luck to both of you, and very best wishes,

Matthew Kelly.

END OF CORRESPONDENCE

Flat 12
Burgess Hill
West Sussex

21 May 2007

Mr Sylvester McCoy
London

Dear Mr McCoy

Ever since I was a young boy I have been a great fan of the legendary *Dr Who*, and you remain my favourite incarnation of the brilliant Time Lord.

Three years ago my interest in *Dr Who* even prompted me to embark on an exciting project. I decided to build a life-sized likeness of the TARDIS in my back garden. Being such a devotee to the TV series, I had intimate knowledge of every tiny detail of the famous Police box and was able to build an exact replica from wood, metal and glass. My TARDIS took four months to create and I was extremely pleased with it. However, the creation of the blue box itself was only the beginning: it was merely the outward representation of something much bigger. To be truly authentic my TARDIS would need to be impossibly larger within than without! This presented quite a challenge but I tackled the task by building a complex of subterranean tunnels some three metres below my lawn and extending over one hundred square metres in total (I got rather carried away).

My calculations show that it even spreads into the grounds of three of my neighbours but its underground concealment allows it to go undetected! The wooden structure above ground has no floor, allowing immediate access to the labyrinth below. Due to constraints imposed by the physical structure of the tunnels I was forced to exercise a degree of creative licence, lining the tunnel-walls with sheets of steel. Blue light filters through holes in the steel to create a very atmospheric hue and sounds effects issue from dozens of hidden speakers. Hideous monsters also lurk in the shadows, their air of menace heightened by the earthworms that burrow within their latex bodies. Recently, a tunnel collapsed, trapping me several metres from the exit, but I managed to dig my way out and later shored up the tunnel with wooden planks. I am confident that it is now safe! Whenever I venture into the bowels of my TARDIS a chill runs down my spine and I feel a profound connection with the Time Lord himself!

I hope you will agree that my TARDIS is quite a feat of engineering. I believe it deserves to be enjoyed by *all Dr Who* fans so I am planning to open it to the general public who would be charged a modest fee (to pay for the TARDIS's maintenance). I would be honoured if you would officially open the site for business. I am sure your involvement would generate some much needed publicity.

I plan to open the TARDIS in September 2007. Please let me know when you would be available. In the meantime, I am commissioning a life-sized cardboard cut-out of you to stand guard at the entrance to my Police box!

I look forward to hearing from you.

Yours truly

J. Henby

NO RESPONSE

Julian Henby

Flat 12
Burgess Hill
West Sussex

21 May 2007

Mr Nick Ross
BBC White City
London W12

Dear Mr Ross

I congratulate you on your fine presenting of *Crimewatch UK* which continues to keep us safe behind our deadlocks and reinforced steel doors.

Over the years I regularly watched your programme with great expectation, looking forward to the end and your immortal catchphrase: 'Don't have nightmares… Do sleep well.' It is regarding this catchphrase that I write to you.

Recently, I was charged with the task of accommodating my younger brother, Dave for two weeks while our mother was camping in the woods with the Buddhists. After the initial settling in period I took to reading a short story to Dave each evening before he went to sleep, introducing him to Stephen King's anthology *The Skeleton Crew*. Please forgive me, Nick, but I have been in the habit of using your catchphrase (without your consent) whenever it seemed fitting. Indeed, it soon became my nightly routine to advise my brother, 'Don't have nightmares… Do sleep well' before switching off his light! This was not merely for my own amusement – it was to keep any unsavoury dreams at bay.

However, I must report that your charm failed to have the expected protective effect on Dave. Three days into his visit I was sitting in the lounge watching a documentary on cross-dressing when I heard a terrible shriek from upstairs. Rushing into my brother's bedroom, I found him sitting on his bed in a cold sweat and pallid. Once he had calmed down he recounted an awful nightmare involving a bearded old man with impossibly elongated legs who was pursuing him through a dark tunnel, babbling incoherently! It seemed undeniably clear that this was a nightmare featuring my Great Uncle Sandy who was in the habit of consuming half a bottle of scotch before rampaging through the streets in search of Nazis.

Despite my great affection for your catchphrase I thought it only fair to express my concern over its effectiveness. I do hope that you will not take this too hard.

Will you be making a public announcement regarding this matter on *Crimewatch* and will you be holding an inquiry?

I look forward to hearing from you.

Yours truly

Julian Henby

Julian Henby

7 September 2007

Julian Henby

Burgess Hill
West Sussex

Dear Mr Henby,

Thank you for your letter, which has taken rather a long time to reach me.

In view of your nephew's poor reaction to the expression, *don't have nightmares*, I have decided to drop it altogether.

With good wishes.

Flat 12
Burgess Hill
West Sussex

21 May 2007

Miss Tara Palmer-Tomkinson
Chelsea

Dear Tara

I have been informed that you are a professional socialite and I therefore approach you with a view to hiring your services.

We are planning an event to celebrate young Tony's initiation into his exclusive club. This will be a fairly modest affair with a small brass band, disco, clay-pigeon shooting on the west lawn, fireworks and a few guest speakers. There will, of course, be food on offer and drinks served from our licensed bar. I have been in contact with Her Majesty The Queen and we are very hopeful that she will honour us with a special message via satellite link on the night.

Your role as a socialite would involve standing around with a glass of Champagne, smiling politely and humouring any libidinal men who chat you up. Approved topics of conversation include yachts, thoroughbred horses and 'those unfortunate working class chaps'.

We are willing to negotiate your fee and I can assure you that you would be paid handsomely.

The event has been scheduled for 14 July. Please confirm whether you wish to take on your role as senior socialite.

I look forward to hearing from you.

Yours truly

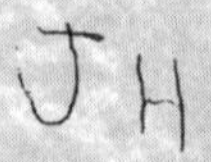

Julian Henby

NO RESPONSE

Flat 12
Burgess Hill
West Sussex

27 November 2006

Sir Cliff Richard
Surrey

Dear Sir Cliff

I write to you regarding something rather disturbing.

I recently downloaded your record 'Living Doll' onto my computer (of course, I paid for it). One of my hobbies is being a DJ. In other words, I like to use special computer software to mix and modify musical tracks, adding different beats, samples, etc.

Anyway, I decided to manipulate 'Living Doll' by slowing it down and playing it in reverse. My plan was to mix it up with some *Eminem* (expletives) and classical music. However, when I reversed the track and slowed it to 26.7% of its normal speed I got quite a shock:

I heard the words 'I love Satan' coming through my PC speakers! The phrase was spoken in a deep, sinister tone that sent a shiver down my spine. The terrible voice repeated its evil mantra over and over until I covered my ears and fled my living room in terror.

I told my mother (who is fanatically religious) about the strange phenomenon and she made me jump into a bath of near-scolding water to be cleansed of evil. She also destroyed my entire CD collection (including my *Meatloaf* records).

Where does this voice come from? Do we require the services of an exorcist?

Yours truly

J. Henby

NO RESPONSE

Julian Henby

Flat 12
Burgess Hill
West Sussex

21 May 2007

Ms Emma Thompson
Fifth Floor
London

Dear Ms Thompson

For the past two years I have been suffering from a terrible affliction that is ruining my life. You may find this hard to believe but I constantly hear Murray Walker's voice inside my head issuing a running commentary on my every move exactly like the main character of your film, *Stranger Than Fiction*. As soon as I awaken in the morning Murray's voice comes in, excitedly announcing the start of a new day and giving a brief recap of the previous night. From that moment onwards there is no letup: I go to the lavatory and the state of my bowels is announced; I take a shower and the speed of my washing is screamed in my ear; the path and handling of my razor as it slides over the contours of my face is discussed at length in Murray's voice! And these are just a few examples.

The psychologists have been unable to help me and the medication prescribed by my doctor has had no effect whatsoever. I am at my wit's end!

If you feel you are able to help in any way I would be most grateful. Was your film based on any real cases? May I see the research?

I would be extremely grateful for any help and anxiously await your response.

Yours truly

Julian Henby

Julian Henby

Dear Julian – as far as I know, my character came entirely out of the writer Zach Helm's head. Perhaps he could help?? You can reach him through the writer's guild of north america. In the meantime, you should probably keep taking the pills.

all the very best –

Emma Thompson

Flat 12
Burgess Hill
West Sussex

10 June 2007

Ms Emma Thompson
Fifth Floor
London

Dear Ms Thompson

Many thanks for your letter.

'You should probably keep taking the pills.' – *why do people keep saying that to me?*

Yours truly

JH

Julian Henby

END OF CORRESPONDENCE

Flat 12
Burgess Hill
West Sussex

21 May 2007

Ms Victoria Wood
London

Dear Ms Wood

I congratulate you on being one of Britain's finest comedians. Not so long ago you made my mother (who is eighty) laugh so much that her teeth fell out and imbedded themselves in a *vol-au-vent*.

Obviously, being a female comedian you have mastered the art of making it in a man's world. I would very much like to hear your thoughts on how you achieved this. Is it tough being a woman on the stand-up circuit?

My enquiry is not driven merely by idle curiosity. You see, I am rather worried about my brother Dave who has now got it into his head that he wants to be a comedian. He recently starred as Eliza in an amateur production of *My Fair Lady* and I must say his success on the stage seems to have gone to his head somewhat, making him believe he is destined to be some kind of bally superstar! As if to compound this ridiculous situation he will insist on wearing ladies' garments all the time and cannot be persuaded to refrain from doing so while auditioning for shows! I am very concerned that poor Dave is setting himself up for a big fall.

I would be most grateful for any advice you can offer on how to help Dave to succeed. Failing that, how might he be persuaded to pull his head from the clouds and be sensible?

I look forward to hearing from you.

Yours truly

Julian Henby

NO RESPONSE

Julian Henby

Association for Diminutive Actors
Flat 12
Burgess Hill
West Sussex

21 May 2007

Mr Nigel Havers
FREEPOST
London

Dear Mr Havers

I have long been a big fan of your brilliant performances on the screen and stage: they provided the inspiration for me to become an actor some three years ago. However, I soon discovered (as I am sure you did) that this business can be particularly tough if you are unusually small. During my three year apprenticeship I struggled to find parts – evidently there is little call for a 4'2' actor! Quite frankly, I am sick of playing a bally dwarf in *Snow White*.

Due to my frustration over the constraints on my expression as an actor, last year I founded the Association for Diminutive Actors (ADA). This is a group set up to lobby production companies for better parts for smaller actors like you and I. We provide our actors with specially trained agents to liase with prospective employers with a view to obtaining equal opportunities. We also hold social events and seminars for members.

Once per month we invite guest speakers to give a short talk on their careers and how they became successful despite their size. We would be honoured to have you as one such guest speaker (we also invite you to join the association).

Please confirm whether you are interested and when you would be free.

Yours truly

Julian Henby

Julian Henby
Founder, ADA

PS. A small step-stool will be provided for you at the podium and you will find all facilities have been adapted to accommodate the smaller person.

Julian Henby,
ADA,

Burgess Hill,
West Sussex

2007-06-23

Dear Mr. Henby,

Nigel Havers has asked me to respond to your letter of 21st May as he is in New York for the next month or so.

He was very flattered to be invited to participate in a forthcoming ADA event, and subject to availability would be happy to do so. On his return from New York, he is filming Tom Thumb, an independent feature for SBPF Films, and is then hoping to take a touring production of Willis Hall's The Long The Short and The Tall into the West End until Christmas. Would early 2008 be good for you?

I shall look forward to hearing from you.

Yours sincerely,

pp Michael Whitehall

MICHAEL WHITEHALL

Association for Diminutive Actors
Flat 12
Burgess Hill
West Sussex

12 July 2007

Mr Nigel Havers
(via Mr Michael Whitehall)
London

Dear Mr Havers

I must congratulate you on landing a part in *The Long, The Short and The Tall*. To my knowledge there are no abnormally short characters in this play so I can only assume you negotiated quite a major change to the script (perhaps it transpires that the Japanese POW was unable to escape due to his short stumpy legs – this would add an interesting twist to the story). Anyway, you would clearly be a great asset to the Association and I am delighted to learn that you are willing to deliver a speech to our members.

Early 2008 would indeed be very convenient for us. We have the luxury of being rather flexible so I suggest you offer a selection of dates for us to choose from and we will fit you in. On 12 February a number of members are attending a seminar titled: 'From The Rack to Stilettos: The History of Height-Gain Therapy', but our schedule is otherwise quite free.

I look forward to hearing from you soon.

Yours truly

JH

END OF CORRESPONDENCE

Julian Henby

Flat 12
Burgess Hill
West Sussex

21 May 2007

Mr Paul McKenna
c/o Paul McKenna Training Ltd
London

Dear Mr McKenna

I am aware that you are probably Britain's best hypnotist and I therefore approach you for help with a problem that has caused me no end of suffering.

You will probably find this extremely difficult to believe but since childhood I have been afflicted with a severe phobia of the colour red. Growing up, I was forced to drop out of school because my classroom was decorated with red and I was too terrified to attend. Later, I had similar problems with employment (on one occasion I had to leave a job because my boss started wearing a red tie and I vomited whenever I saw him). Learning to drive was a disaster too because I kept speeding past red traffic lights in terror. My personal life has also been devastated. Several years ago I fell in love with a waitress from Surrey. We courted for several months before deciding to consummate our relationship at a five-star hotel. All was fine until she stripped off to reveal her red underwear. I fled the room screaming and we have not spoken since.

I have now taken to wearing special shaded spectacles that render me virtually blind and walking with a white stick. This is the only way I can be sure of avoiding the colour red. I have had enough of this problem, I must cure it before I do something silly.

Can you help me, please? How do we proceed?

I look forward to hearing from you.

Yours truly

J. Henby

Julian Henby

NO RESPONSE

Flat 12
Burgess Hill
West Sussex

21 May 2007

Ms Edwina Currie
London

Dear Ms Currie

I followed your political career over the years and then your shift into the world of literature. I have come to trust your judgement and therefore hope you will be able to advise me on a very delicate matter.

Some time ago my fiancée Rebecca left me and nothing I do seems to change her opinion of me as some kind of pariah from whom she must maintain a safe distance! Having imbued many of your fictional characters with a talent for the art of seduction you must surely be an expert. I would be most grateful for any advice you can offer me on how to win my Rebecca back. I suspect it cannot merely be a matter of smearing perfume between one's breasts!

Your advice would mean the world to me.

I look forward to hearing from you soon.

Yours truly

J. Henby

Julian Henby

NO RESPONSE

Flat 12
Burgess Hill
West Sussex

21 May 2007

Mr Phillip Schofield
Guildford

Dear Mr Schofield

It is with great fondness that I remember watching you present Children's BBC in your 'broom cupboard' each evening. Back then I was a young lad and you provided a very welcome distraction from all the traumas of childhood.

Your excellent service as a children's television presenter had a profound effect on me and, now in my thirties, I feel it is time to pay homage to you. Therefore, I have spent the past six months building an exact replica of your 'broom cupboard'. Using old videos and information online, every detail has been faithfully recreated. The centrepiece (of which I am immensely proud) is a life-sized waxwork model of you behind your desk. The model was commissioned at great expense and worth every penny as I believe it to be a perfect likeness! Your partner Gordon the Gopher was rather less costly but is an equally faithful representation.

My plan is to open the replica broom cupboard to the general public some time next year. I believe it deserves to be seen by anyone who wants to view it and this would be a fitting celebration of your work. Before beginning work on the promotion of the museum there is one detail that needs attending to. I wish to install a speaker via which interesting information about your broom cupboard could be conveyed to the visitors. I would like my waxwork model to communicate the information so the model really needs to possess your voice. I would therefore be extremely honoured if you would kindly record the information and phrases (which I will supply) onto compact disc. I will naturally provide all recording equipment and pay you for your time.

Please confirm whether you are willing to lend your voice to my museum piece. I would also be honoured to have you open my broom cupboard to the public.

Yours truly

Julian Henby

NO RESPONSE

Julian Henby

Flat 12
Burgess Hill
West Sussex

18 July 2007

Mr Richard Stilgoe
Orpheus Centre
Surrey

Dear Mr Stilgoe

Firstly, I congratulate you on your illustrious career in show business. Bravo!

Now to get to the point. I have been a semi-professional inventor for several years and my latest invention might very well be of interest to you. It is an entirely innovative musical instrument that does not require hands, feet (or limb-extensions of any kind) to play! The instrument (which I am calling the *Oralyricsynth*) has been developed with the help of a professional musician who has been quoted as saying that the design 'will surely herald a revolution within the music industry'.

I will not disclose any further details of my *Oralyricsynth* at this point in case you are not interested. However, I would like to send you a pictorial description of the design for your scrutiny. I am sure any ideas you might have for improvements to the instrument would be absolutely invaluable.

Please let me know whether you are interested.

I look forward to hearing from you soon.

Yours truly

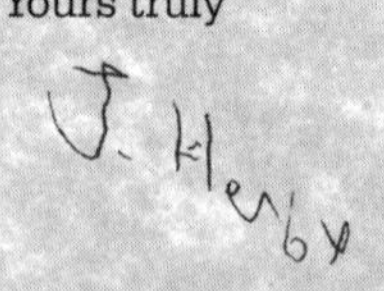

Julian Henby

Mr Julian Henby

7 August, 2007

Hants

Dear Julian Henby,

Richard has asked me to thank you for your letter of the 18th July. Sorry for the delay in replying but he has been on holiday.

He would, indeed, be interested to have more details of your *Oralyricsynth* because as you know we have some quite severely disabled young people at The Orpheus Centre who may benefit from such an instrument.

We look forward to hearing from you again.

Best wishes,

Jenny Bond
PA to **RICHARD STILGOE**

COMMUNITY FUND
Lottery money making a difference

Royal Patron: HRH The Earl of Wessex KCVO
Patron: Dr Michael Swallow OBE FRCP
Founder: Richard Stilgoe OBE DL
Registered Charity No. 292501

Flat 12
Burgess Hill
West Sussex

11 August 2007

Mr Richard Stilgoe
Orpheus Centre
Surrey

Dear Mr Stilgoe

Many thanks for your letter (via Jenny Bond) of 7 August. I am very pleased that you are interested in having more details of my invention – the *Oralyricsynth*. Please find enclosed a pictorial description of the system. The design continues to evolve and we are very open to any suggestions for improvements so please feel free to suggest any refinements.

I would like to bring a prototype down to your Orpheus centre for a demonstration. Please do let me know when this would be convenient.

We are also starting up a campaign to generate interest within the music industry. I am sure your input would give the campaign a huge boost. It would be an honour to have you as a speaker at some of our demonstrations. I have also been in touch with various media organisations and we are hopeful of stimulating a good deal of publicity. I trust you would have no objections if I were to report that you (the great Richard Stilgoe) are working with me to penetrate the musical mainstream with the *Oralyricsynth* – your support will certainly lend credibility to the campaign!

I look forward to hearing from you soon.

Yours truly

JH

Julian Henby

# Oralyricsynth - The Revolutionary New Musical Instrument

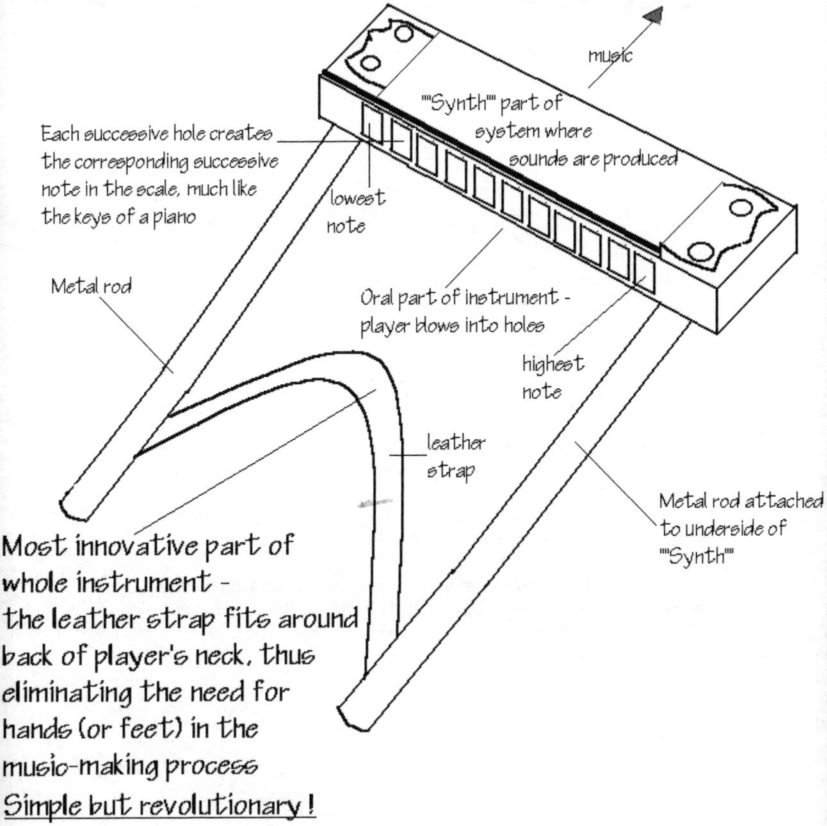

music

""Synth"" part of
system where
sounds are produced

Each successive hole creates
the corresponding successive
note in the scale, much like
the keys of a piano

lowest
note

Metal rod

Oral part of instrument -
player blows into holes

highest
note

leather
strap

Metal rod attached
to underside of
""Synth""

Most innovative part of
whole instrument -
the leather strap fits around
back of player's neck, thus
eliminating the need for
hands (or feet) in the
music-making process
Simple but revolutionary !

Intelectual property of Julian Henby & Tony Bellows 2004-2007 - patents pending

Mr Julian Henby

Hants

16 August, 2007

Dear Julian,

Thank you for sending me the picture. This feels terribly like a wind-up. I and thousands like me have for years been playing a mouth organ on a mouth organ holder. Look at: www.stairwaytokevin.com>harmonica/mouthorganaccessories. How does what you have invented differ from this?

Meanwhile, under no circumstances must you assume that I am involved in this. I am sorry to sound negative, and I hope I am wrong about the originality of the design.

Yours sincerely,

Richard Stilgoe

**RICHARD STILGOE**

END OF CORRESPONDENCE

COMMUNITY FUND
Lottery money making a difference

Royal Patron: HRH The Earl of Wessex KCVO
Patron: Dr Michael Swallow OBE FRCP
Founder: Richard Stilgoe OBE DL
Registered Charity No. 292501

Flat 12
Burgess Hill
West Sussex

8 July 2007

Mr Alan Davies
London

Dear Alan

I am a big fan of your television programme, *Jonathan Creek*. However, on this occasion I am writing to you regarding a personal matter.

I recently read a magazine article claiming that you gave up a life of crime to pursue a career in show business and comedy. This set of circumstances makes you uniquely qualified to assist with a rather delicate problem concerning my brother. On a recent shopping trip with my brother I had reason to visit my local Barclays Bank after which we enjoyed a pleasant afternoon buying groceries. However, upon our return I discovered several biros secreted in the little bag that my brother carries everywhere. Upon close inspection the blue pens revealed themselves to be the property of one Barclays Bank. My brother Dave must have swiped them when nobody was watching and hidden them in his bag!

Fearing for Dave's safety, I decided not to return the pens to the bank and instead disposed of them in a local pond (please do not tell the police, Alan). I have also been keeping the secret of my brother's crime from my mother – a secret that is eating me alive. I am desperate to protect my poor brother from the horrors of prison.

I am terrified that Dave has wandered onto the slippery slope to a life of crime. This is probably a brazen imposition, but would you be prepared to come to my flat and speak to him? Perhaps if you told the story of how you went to the brink of self-destruction before seeing the light, this would shock him into changing his ways. I will pay you whatever I can.

I look forward to hearing from you soon.

Yours truly

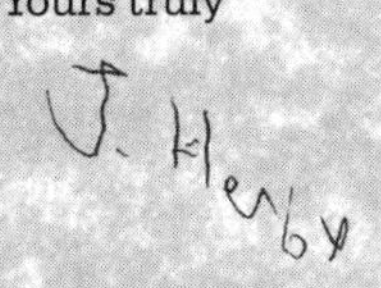

Julian Henby

Flat 12
Burgess Hill
West Sussex

8 July 2007

Ms Anneka Rice
Performing Artistes
Surrey

Dear Ms Rice

I have long been a big fan of yours and particularly enjoyed your television programme, *Challenge Anneka*. It is regarding this show that I write to you.

My younger brother Dave can be rather lazy at times and frequently spends lengthy periods playing his video games or watching television when he should be tidying his bedroom or performing some other chore.

Recently he stayed at my flat for six weeks while our mother went camping with the Buddhists. During this period I did my utmost to ensure that he maintained high standards of self-responsibility: he was instructed to carry out basic cleaning, laundry and even catering tasks. On the many occasions when he took to his computer instead of the dishwasher, I provided him with motivation:

'If you don't do your chore', I told him, 'I'll phone up *Challenge Anneka* and she'll be round with a posse of burly men to whip you into shape!' This became my standard threat and I issued it with great frequency even doing so before extinguishing my brother's bedroom light at bed-time.

One fateful night I was woken by a noise. Rushing outside I was confronted by a mob of drunken yobs who were smashing beer bottles and generally spoiling the restful ambience of the street. A blonde woman with tattoos egged on the uncivilised men, issuing orders to perpetrate further criminal acts. One such order was to vandalise my front door and the yobs promptly obeyed, continuing their work even when I had retreated inside.

It later transpired that Dave had witnessed the whole event from his bedroom window and had been severely traumatised. Further, he was convinced that we had just been attacked by Anneka Rice and her posse of burly men!

During the days following the attack my brother became incredibly diligent with his chores, prompting me to refrain from correcting his mistake. However, I am now suffering a crisis of conscience over my decision. Now that he is back at my mother's house, Dave remains traumatised: he suffers frequent nightmares about *Challenge Anneka* and grows more withdrawn by the day. My flat may be spotless but I wonder if the price was too high!

Would you be prepared to meet my mother and Dave to straighten this whole mess out? I feel this is the only possible solution without which my brother will certainly self-destruct! When would you be free?

Yours truly

J. Henby

Julian Henby

NO RESPONSE

Flat 12
Burgess Hill
West Sussex

8 July 2007

Mr Keith Chegwin
London

Dear Mr Chegwin

I am organising an event to raise money for charity. In part, the event has been inspired by your brilliant career as children's game-show host: influenced by your classic pop quiz, the charity event is called *Preggers Play Pop*! The format is as follows:

It is hoped the event will take place in the maternity ward of a London hospital. Paying spectators will assemble in the ward where a group of eight pregnant women (in the throes of labour) will form the cornerstone of the show. Three spectators will be invited to become contestants, each competing for a prize. The contestants must start by interviewing each woman in turn to obtain useful information. Upon completion of these interviews each contestant is to decide which prospective mother will give birth first and place a bet of cash upon that woman! The winner will be awarded half the winnings while the other half is donated to charity.

The event, of course, requires an enthusiastic host to whip the crowd up into a frenzy, interview the contestants and make fun of the women giving birth. I would be honoured to have you as that host. I am sure you will agree it is for a good cause.

Please confirm whether you are able to take part and when you would be available.

I look forward to hearing from you.

Yours truly

Julian Henby

NO RESPONSE

Julian Henby

Flat 12
Burgess Hill
West Sussex

8 July 2007

Mr Adam Hart-Davis
c/o UKTV (History)
160 Great Portland Street
London W1W 5QA

Dear Adam

I am a big fan of your television series on British history and write to you for your expertise.

Studying for a college course, I am required to write an essay on World War II analysing the traumas endured by civilians living in Britain. One area of interest was, of course, the strategy of 'blackouts'. I recently read an online article that mentioned the fact that bald-headed men were obliged to wear hats during the blackout to minimise the risk of light being reflected off their heads and alerting German bombers to their presence. Before reading the article I had never heard of this and I found it rather intriguing. Unfortunately, the 'hat rule' was only mentioned briefly and I have not been able to find any further information on it.

I would be most grateful if you would kindly provide me with some information on the 'hat rule' or send me a list of relevant publications. I am very interested to know whether there was widespread obedience by bald men or whether they rebelled, perhaps even polishing their scalps with beeswax in a show of defiance!

Any information would be very gratefully received. I look forward to hearing from you.

Yours truly

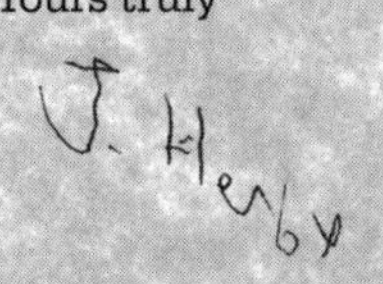

NO RESPONSE

Julian Henby

Flat 12
Burgess Hill
West Sussex

21 May 2007

Ms Joanna Lumley
London

Dear Joanna

My elderly uncle lives in a nursing home and considers you something of a pin-up girl. He and his friends are too old to write to you unfortunately (some can hardly see through their cataracts). They have therefore asked me to drop you a line asking whether you would be prepared to visit the nursing home (in Hampshire) and give a little talk about your life and career. I am sure your visit would brighten up their day no end.

Please let me know when you would be available. We can fit you in almost anytime – the old boys have quite a free schedule!

I look forward to hearing from you soon.

Yours truly

Julian Henby

Julian Henby

JOANNA LUMLEY

31 May 2007

Jear Mr Henby,

oanna Lumley has asked me to thank you so very much for your letter of :1st May inviting her to visit your uncle's nursing home to give a talk .bout her life and career, but to tell you she very much regrets that she is ınable to accept your kind invitation as her diary is completely full for he foreseeable future.

Aiss Lumley sends her warmest good wishes to you and your uncle and ll his friends in the nursing home.

Yours sincerely,

Lisa Baker

PA to Miss Lumley

Flat 12
Burgess Hill
West Sussex

5 June 2007

Ms Joanna Lumley
London

Dear Joanna

Many thanks for your letter (via Lisa Baker) of 31 May. We were all quite disappointed to learn that you are unable to visit my uncle and his chums in the nursing home.

I am afraid when I informed the old boys that I had written the invitation to you they got rather carried away and obtained a large quantity of Viagra tablets (illegally). The ringleader is now in police custody and the others (including my uncle) are facing eviction from the nursing home! There have also been a number of injuries (knocks and bruises) resulting from the chaps ingesting some of the pills for 'test purposes'.

I wonder if you would be prepared to explain the reasons for this incident to the police and put in a good word for the poor old chaps. After all, they were only responding to their excitement over your hoped-for visit.

Yours truly

JH

Julian Henby

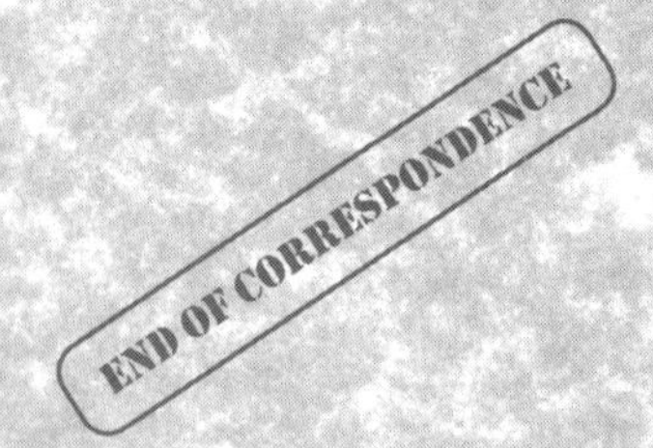

Flat 12
Burgess Hill
West Sussex

8 July 2007

Mr Brian May
The Official International Queen Fan Club
London

Dear Mr May

I have been a big fan of *Queen* for many years and continued to follow your solo career after the tragic death of Freddie Mercury.

For some eight years now I have been a struggling musician. I have been a member of three different bands and played many gigs across the country. Two years ago I abandoned my keyboard and decided to learn the lead guitar instead. I purchased a used electric guitar from a local shop and, after several months of practice, became quite proficient. Not long ago I even started taking my guitar on stage. It was all going extremely well: I was happy with my choice of instrument; the audiences liked it; and I was exhilarated! However, a few weeks ago something strange happened.

Being such a Queen devotee, I naturally spend a lot of time playing your songs on my guitar. One evening at dusk I was playing *The Great Pretender* in my garden. It was a beautiful guitar solo but I was imagining an accompaniment inside by head, my eyes squeezed shut. The song and the moving sound of the guitar sent me into a kind of trance and I felt I was floating on thin air. Then something really strange happened: the voice of Freddie Mercury himself started to come from the speaker of my amp! The great Freddie Mercury was actually singing with me, providing lead vocals! Despite feeling shocked to my core I continued to play the song to the end, mesmerised and unable to stop. When the number finally did end and the last note dissolved into the evening, there came an unnatural hush: even the birds fell silent. I felt momentarily paralysed, transfixed by awe!

Following that incredible evening I became too scared to play my guitar and it lay untouched for three days. Eventually, I mustered the courage to start playing it again but Freddie did not return. I have now taken to playing the guitar regularly once more. However, the thought of playing a concert fills me with dread. What if Freddie returns? How will the audience react? I fear that I shall never be able to do another gig and my career as a musician is over.

I write to you for help. Has Freddie ever come to you through your guitar? How should I deal with this bizarre situation? I know this is hard to believe, but I assure you it is all true. I am desperate to get back on stage. Please help.

Yours truly

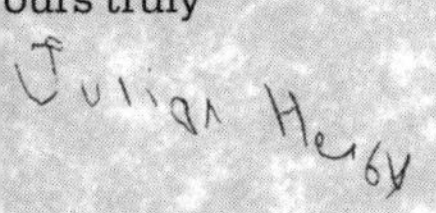

Julian Henby

Flat 12
Burgess Hill
West Sussex

23 February 2007

Mr Richard Wilson
London

Dear Mr Wilson

My uncle Warren was a great fan of your comedy programme *One Foot In The Grave*. In fact, he was so taken with the character of Victor Meldrew that he could often be heard shouting '*I don't believe it!*' from his bedroom window in Slough (on one occasion he was heard by a group of drunken youths who responded by smashing his windows).

I know that one of Warren's greatest wishes was to meet you, but unfortunately he passed away last month. However, my aunt Ruth (Warren's widow) recently had a brilliant idea: Why don't we commission a lifelike wax model of Warren to be featured in a future episode of *One Foot In The Grave*? So that is what we are doing. Using dozens of photographs and measurements of Warren, a life-sized wax model (much like those seen in London's Madame Tussauds) is being created.

We would very much appreciate it if your writers could produce a script featuring Victor Meldrew asleep or unconscious for at least 50% of the episode so that Warren can play Victor from beyond the grave. Unfortunately, he does not closely resemble Victor Meldrew (he is black) but I am confident this could be overcome with the clever use of makeup and a cloth cap.

I do hope you can help. It would mean a lot to aunt Ruth.

Yours truly

Julian Henby

Julian Henby

# RICHARD WILSON

16 March 2007

Julian Henby
Flat 12

Burgess Hill
West Sussex

Dear Julian

Thank you very much for your letter of 23 February.

I applaud your efforts to preserve the memory of your uncle Warren. However, they are all in vain as there will be no more *One Foot in the Grave.* The writer has hung up his pens and cannot be coaxed to change his mind.

Sorry about that.

Best wishes

Richard Wilson

Flat 12
Burgess Hill
West Sussex

21 March 2007

Mr Richard Wilson
London

Dear Richard

Many thanks for your letter of 16 March.

I was very disappointed to learn that there will be no new episodes of *One Foot in the Grave*. This news has dealt a particularly heavy blow to poor Aunt Ruth who had her heart set on fulfilling her late husband's dream to appear (in wax form) on the show. When I broke the bad news to her, Ruth slipped into an awful depression that lasted all day.

The waxwork model of my Uncle Warren is now virtually complete and the artist emailed a set of photos to us only today. I must say, Richard, the model is incredibly lifelike and could almost be Warren himself! In fact, it is such a good likeness that poor Ruth became rather upset when she saw it. Obviously, it is too late to cancel the commission and it will cost us rather a lot of money. This is all such a wretched mess and all my fault for encouraging Ruth to do it!

I feel there is only one way to salvage something from this whole mess: If you were prepared to meet Warren (the model) and be photographed with him I am sure this would mean the world to Aunt Ruth. Hopefully, this would adequately compensate her for the bitter disappointment she has suffered.

Would you be willing to consider doing this for us? It would be an enormous honour for Ruth and I feel it would help to mend her broken heart.

I look forward to hearing from you.

Yours truly

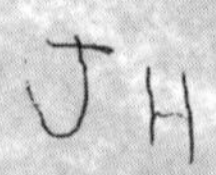

Julian Henby

Flat 12
Burgess Hill
West Sussex

8 July 2007

Lulu
London

Dear Lulu

I consider myself to be your greatest fan and have been for some time. Over one decade ago I met you and you were good enough to sign your name across my abdomen with a permanent marker pen. Since then I have taken incredible care to ensure the autograph remains perfectly preserved. I have not washed my torso since the wonderful day of our meeting. I also wear ice-packs over my clothes to prevent sweating and avoid rainwater at all costs. Sometimes the signature seems to fade so I am forced to touch it up with a permanent marker, much as an art restorer would.

My reward for all these measures is the perfectly intact original autograph of the best singer of all time! However, my former fiancée Rebecca failed to see the significance of this: she left me some months ago, citing my refusal to wash as a major factor in her decision.

Would you be prepared to speak to Rebecca and make her see how unreasonable she is being? I would be most grateful for your intervention – I need my Rebecca back!

I look forward to hearing from you soon.

Yours truly

Julian Henby

NO RESPONSE

Julian Henby
(your number 1 fan)

Flat 12
Burgess Hill
West Sussex

29 January 2007

To: The King

You have pulled the wool over nearly everyone's eyes, but you cannot fool a dedicated fan like me! I know you didn't really die on 16 August 1977 while sitting on your toilet seat in Memphis. Perhaps you thought that, after all this time, no one would notice you slipping out of the USA and getting a managerial job at a Café Bar in Sussex, UK. Well, Elvis, I have been onto you for some time and your cover is blown.

Why did you fake your own death? How could you do that to your adoring fans? I suppose you had your reasons and presumably you wish to remain hidden (otherwise you would have revealed yourself). I will therefore keep the secret of your existence, but I implore you to come out of hiding and meet your fans!

Can we meet at the Café Bar so I can see for myself that it's really you? When are you free?

(By the way, do you know where Marilyn Monroe is living these days? Does she still have that hair salon in Newbury?)

I await your response.

*Thank you very much,*

J. Henby

Julian Henby

at 12

urgess Hill
'est Sussex

ear Julian

simply can not believe after all these years my cover has been blown.

ow did you track me down? I have managed to deny my urges and have not played ny music for nearly 30 years. I can only imagine my evil temptations got the better f me and you recognised Burning Love on the ring tone of my mobile phone. How tupid could I have been? I urge you to keep this information to yourself.

ly identity is critical to my life. I could not go back to the previous life or torture, eing subjected to daily abuse with woman throwing themselves at my on every orner. Should you wish to meet I can arrange this. I will explain all, you will be the irst and only person to know Elvis real story.

lease come alone. I will meet you at midnight on Thursday at the dark alley behind he bar. Do not tell anyone about our meeting. You will recognise me in the long dark rench coat with the baseball bat and sawn off shotgun (if I can get one in time).

Yours faithfully

The King

PS – Marilyn is living nearby in another bar, dressed and living as a man in very tight trousers

Flat 12
Burgess Hill
West Sussex

8 July 2007
18 March 2007

King Elvis

Dear Elvis Presley (the King)

Thank you for your letter. We are kindred spirits – I too know the constant torment of women throwing themselves at me wherever I go. It is the price we must pay, Elvis, for our supernatural animal magnetism.

I will be at your specified venue on Thursday for our meeting. From your letter I am assuming you will have baseball practice (and clay pigeon shooting) immediately afterward so I shall be punctual.

Do not fear, Elvis – your secret is safe.

Yours truly

JH

Julian Henby

PS Could you introduce Marilyn Monroe to my brother (Dave)? I feel they would make a good couple.

# ABOUT THE AUTHOR

The letters in this book are so absurd that the author could not bring himself to sign them with his own name. In fact, Henby is a pseudonym of Julian Henley.

In real life, Julian Henley (the man behind Henby) graduated from the University of Brighton with a Postgraduate Diploma in Counselling and is now a highly qualified humanistic counsellor. He has worked with clients from all walks of life but initially specialised in counselling people with drug and alcohol addictions.

Julian has cerebral palsy and is seriously considering getting his wheelchair turbo-charged to outrun any disgruntled celebrities…